THE PEDALER'S HANDBOOK

Jeffrey Blish

THE PEDALER'S HANDBOOK:
A Guide for Bicyclists

Illustrations by Marilyn Steiner

NASH PUBLISHING · LOS ANGELES

Copyright©1972 by Nash Publishing

All rights reserved. No part of this book
may be reproduced in any form or by any means
without permission in writing from the publisher.

Library of Congress Catalog Card Number: 70-186917
Standard Book Number: 8402-8033-5

Published simultaneously in the United States and Canada
by Nash Publishing Corporation, 9255 Sunset Boulevard,
Los Angeles, California 90069.

Printed in the United States of America.

First Printing.

Contents

1. Introduction *3*
2. Buyer's Guide *11*
3. Accessories *23*
4. Learning to Ride *37*
5. Getting in Shape *45*
6. Rules of the Road *59*
7. Picking Local Routes *67*
8. Preparing for a Trip *71*
9. Hosteling *83*
10. Know the Way *91*
11. Buying a Used Bicycle *99*
12. Repair Guide *109*
13. Gearing *123*

14. Racing and Endurance Contests   *129*
15. Camp Cooking   *137*
16. First Aid   *147*
17. Dos and Don'ts   *161*
18. Keep it Clean   *167*
19. Protect Your Property   *179*
20. Traveling with Your Bike   *185*
21. Checklists   *191*
22. Appendix   *197*
23. Index   *203*

THE PEDALER'S HANDBOOK

Chapter 1

Introduction

During recent years, there has been a steady increase in the popularity of bicycling. As more and more people of all ages are discovering the many pleasures and advantages of owning their own bicycle, more and more bicycle dealers are struggling to keep up with the rise in demand. There is good reason for this trend. Bicycling represents a unique blend of utility and pleasure requiring a minimum amount of skill and can be mastered easily by a variety of people for a variety of purposes. It is a sport in which the entire family, young and old alike, can participate. The bicycle is also an effective and inexpensive means of transportation which can open up a whole new world of sights and sounds that would otherwise remain undiscovered.

WHY BICYCLE?: This being the age of the internal combustion engine, many people tend to look upon the bicycle either as a toy for children or as a means of transportation reserved for those not yet old enough to drive an automobile. For many it is a childhood memory that was traded in for a four-wheeler with hundreds of horsepower upon coming of age. However, in actuality, the bicycle is a much-needed alternative to the many disadvantages of the automobile. If the popularity of bicycling continues to rise it could do much to reduce the amount of pollution in the air we breathe and afford relief from the nerve-wracking congestion on our city streets. Instead of the tension and mental fatigue experienced after a drive through city traffic, cyclists would arrive at their destinations feeling relaxed and alert.

Since there is virtually no exercise involved in driving an automobile, bicycles have done much to promote the health and well-being of those individuals who have discovered that a bicycle is more than a toy. Millions have already freed themselves from the metal confines of their automobiles, and are enjoying hour after hour of pleasant communication with their surroundings while going about the everyday business of traveling from one place to another.

Even if the automobile is a necessary evil, as I suppose it is, the bicycle can still play an important role in improving the life of almost anyone. Everyone, young and old, can benefit from an occasional outing with their bicycle. A Sunday ride or a weekend camping excursion can at least leave you feeling fit and ready to face your Monday-morning automobile with a healthy body and an alert mind. A ride in the evening can do much to relieve the tensions and frustrations that build up so readily during the course of the day. If you are still not convinced that bicycling is for you, perhaps a detailed discussion of the many advantages that are awaiting you may change your mind.

INTRODUCTION

HEALTH: Good health is something that can be enjoyed and should be sought by everyone. There is no more enjoyable way of attaining good health than on a bicycle. One hour of bicycling provides just the right amount of physical exertion required for effective exercise without the drudgery inherent in most exercise programs.

Bicycling is an effective way of improving the body's blood circulation. The blood is the medium by which the body is supplied with oxygen and nutrition. Poor circulation of the blood can impair the functioning of the cells in every part of the human body. It can cause the brain to operate below its normal capacity. It can make a person feel slow and sluggish. During a period of physical exertion such as bicycling, the cells of the body are required to work at full capacity. This means that the blood must circulate faster in order to supply the cells with the oxygen needed to maintain a peak output. The human body is a remarkable machine that operates at a higher level of efficiency than any yet invented by man, yet it is a machine that must be used if it is to maintain that efficiency. If your body consistently works at its lowest capacity, as it does most of the time, it will not be capable of performing in situations that require a greater output of energy. It will also operate at a lower level of efficiency during periods of normal activity. If you feel run-down, it is probably an accurate description of exactly what you are. With good blood circulation, your body is always ready and able to perform to whatever capacity is needed, and bicycling is one of the best ways to ensure good circulation.

Better circulation can also reduce the possibility of vascular disease. Heart attacks and strokes are the number-one cause of death year after year, and many prominent doctors advocate bicycling, specifically, as a prevention against heart ailments. Our lives are filled with extended periods of inactivity, and inactivity weakens the heart, leaving most people prone to heart problems. A good bicycling program can provide relief from this devastating inactivity and add years to an individual's life expectancy.

Inactivity also contributes to poor muscle tone in the body. It can leave a person weak and highly susceptible to bruises, pulled muscles, and general aches and pains. Many people who consider themselves slightly overweight are really victims of sagging muscles. A good bicycling program can trim down those muscles and keep them fit. Bicycling is especially good for back muscles. It has been said that humans made a mistake when they stood upright. Man, more than any other animal, is plagued by back troubles, and a bicycle can help prevent all of them. If it is all you can do to get your muscles to drag you home at the end of the day, get yourself a bicycle, and you will be amazed to find that your body feels lighter and that you have developed a spring in your step once again.

If you find yourself winded after climbing a flight of stairs, or panting heavily after running two blocks to catch a bus, you are probably not breathing properly and have a very shallow lung capacity. The lungs and the bloodstream must work together efficiently to supply your body with oxygen. If the lungs cannot furnish enough oxygen to the blood, your body must exert itself beyond its capability during periods of stress. Once again your bicycle can come to the aid of your body by markedly increasing your lungs' capacity. Your lungs should operate with ease at all times. Breathing should be deep and relaxed, except, of course, during periods of exertion, in which case the lungs should be able to operate at the increased rate that is required. The ability to breathe properly is an important part of physical fitness.

Exercise is also instrumental in promoting sound, healthy sleep. I'm sure you have never thought of a bicycle as a cure for insomnia, yet it is the safest, most effective cure in

INTRODUCTION

existence. A good, healthy ride in the evening can relax the muscles of the body, which tend to remain tense after the day's activities. It will make your body feel pleasantly tired without feeling overworked and will relieve the aches and pains which prevent good sleep. It can also take your mind off your everyday problems to ride smoothly past the scenes along your route. With a clear mind and a relaxed feeling in your body, you will be ready to sleep comfortably and soundly. A good night's sleep will leave you wide-awake, alert, and ready to tackle the problems of the following day with ease.

Before leaving the subject of exercise I should say that a good exercise program is one that starts well within the capacities and limitations of the individual. No one can achieve good health his first day out. So go slow, and let your body become accustomed to the demands that will be made on it before you actually make them. Starting too fast can do more harm than good. If you are unsure just how much exercise you should start with, consult your family doctor and he will advise you as to how much is safe for you.

SIGHTSEEING: Another benefit your bicycle will give you is an unlimited view of all the sights your eyes can possibly encompass while on a sightseeing excursion. There is no better way to take in scenery than by the luxury of your own pedal power. If you have ever taken a Sunday drive in your automobile, you have probably discovered that your view is limited somewhat by the speed with which you must view whatever it is you plan to see. If you chanced to slow down long enough to get a good look at anything, you probably encountered an angry motorist honking behind you, who wasn't really interested in the scenery and made it quite definite that he wasn't. Of course you could always park your car and walk around for awhile, that is if you can find a parking space. On a bicycle, sights can be taken in at a leisurely pace, totally independent of the motorists who are in a hurry to reach their destinations. You can stop and start with ease, spending as much time as you like on every item of interest. The parking problem, of course, is greatly alleviated. Any unused tree is parking space enough for a bicycle.

A bicycle carrier mounted on your automobile makes it possible to take in even those sights that are miles away from where you live. Once you reach the area you want to explore, you have only to find one suitable parking space and then proceed on your tour by bike. The greater mobility and the greater freedom to view the sights will undoubtedly increase your pleasure from the places of interest you visit. With your bicycle it is also possible to reach areas that are not readily accessible by automobile.

Of course, one doesn't have to travel far away to find exciting sights. There are probably many exciting things within easy biking distance from where you live that you have never even noticed. A new world can open up right in your own backyard when viewed from a bicycle.

DISADVANTAGES: The major drawback to riding a bicycle is the fact that society is not really geared to the bicyclist. With a few exceptions, streets do not provide a safe and convenient lane for the cyclist, forcing him to fend for himself on roads that were built for the exclusive use of the automobile. Many cities do not provide bicycle racks for parking bicycles. Although some cities have provided bicycle paths on city property and in public parks and some have closed off certain streets on certain days to automobiles allowing cyclists to ride uninhibited by the usual traffic, there is still a need for much more to be done. Many organizations are currently working on this problem and, more and more, cities are realizing the need for bicycle accommodations. However, it will be many years before bicyclists are able to travel the city without having to fight

INTRODUCTION

for space. It is possible to get around, if not comfortably at least safely, under existing conditions. Exactly how this is done will be discussed in a later chapter.

Perhaps the worst problem that will be encountered by the bicyclist is the experience of becoming an avid and insufferable enthusiast. Your friends will be beleaguered by your ceaseless praise of the sport. Your family will be forced to trudge along through many a weekend outing. But take heart! Once they, too, have discovered the joys, the feeling of health, and the friendly spirit which surrounds cyclists, you will have made converts who will be just as enthusiastic as you are.

JUST PLAIN FUN: With all this talk about the many practical advantages of bicycling, it is easy to overlook the simplest benefit of all: bicycling is just plain fun. The feeling of freedom and activity, the pleasant scenery, and the comradery found with other bike enthusiasts will give every bicycle owner hours and hours of enduring pleasure. And what better reason for doing anything?

Chapter 2

Buyer's Guide

Buying a bicycle is not an easy task these days. If you have already walked into a bicycle shop, you will understand what this means. If you haven't started looking yet, you will soon discover why. There are literally hundreds of makes and models to choose from. You will be confronted with different types and sizes of bicycles, all of which come with a varied assortment of handlebars, brakes, gears, tires, and accessories. There will also be a varied assortment of price tags. To choose your bicycle wisely, you will have to be equipped with some knowledge of what bicycles there are and which ones might interest you.

TYPES: Although it is still possible to buy a ballon-tired, single-speed backbuster, I will not discuss this bicycle at all.

If you wanted merely to ride around the block once a day, it would probably be adequate (provided your block was not hilly). These bicycles have been relegated almost exclusively to the use of children—and even most children have abandoned them for multi-speed bicycles with high-rise handlebars. Unless you are under nine years of age and just learning, you should not consider buying a single-speed bicycle.

If you want a bicycle to use for commuting to work and back or for running around the neighborhood, you may want to buy one with a multi-speed rear hub. These bicycles, deceptively called "tourist" or "English racers," are sturdy and provide a secure ride through all kinds of weather. They require less adjustment and maintenance than the more expensive ten-speed bicycles, and their clincher tires are heavier and less prone to have flats; they also have a surer grip on the road for riding in the rain. These bikes come equipped with either three or five speeds, which will enable you to climb hills, and when equipped with front caliper brakes they will be more than adequate for riding short distances.

Though English racers are satisfactory for commuter transportation, they are not well-suited for longer rides. If you plan to use your bicycle for anything other than transportation, you should seriously consider investing your money in a ten-speed derailleur bicycle. Even for transportation, this bicycle would be much easier to ride, being far lighter and easier for climbing hills. Because of the difficulty inherent in riding an English racer, if you end up by buying one you may never want to participate in some of the more enjoyable activities open to the cyclist. Don't be discouraged by the difficulty of riding a heavy machine before you have ridden a ten-speed lightweight. Before you decide to buy a bicycle you should try riding both types. You will notice the difference in the ease of cycling immediately. If there is any possibility that you will want to do any extensive cycling, and you should consider it, you will need a ten-speed.

The ten-speed bicycle is lightweight and equipped with a derailleur gear-changer mechanism that gives the cyclist a choice of ten different gear ratios. This selection of gears and their light weight make these bicycles easy to ride and suitable for traveling long distances, including up and down hills, without extreme fatigue.

WEIGHT: The weight of your bicycle is one of the most important factors to consider when shopping around. The more a bicycle weighs, the more you will have to work to get it rolling. Advances have been made in the development of stronger materials that enable manufacturers to produce bicycle frames of extremely light weight and with better resiliency than the bicycles of yesteryear. Generally speaking, the more you spend on your bicycle, the less it will weigh.

The highest priced ten-speed bicycles (over $200) will usually weigh between twenty and twenty-five pounds. This is a light bicycle and, if you can afford one, it will offer no resistance to your efforts on the pedals. Medium priced ten-speeds weigh from twenty-five to thirty pounds and cost between $100 and $150. These bicycles, though not as light as the more expensive varieties, are more than adequate and will prevent you from tiring out after the first few miles of riding. The English racers usually weigh between thirty and forty pounds. This is a lot of weight to be pedaling around if you have any distance to ride, especially with the limited selection of gear ratios.

SIZE: Another thing to consider, regardless of the type of bicycle you decide to buy, is the size. Bicycles come in different frame sizes, and you will have to know the size to suit your height. The frame size of a bicycle is measured from the center of the crank to the top of the vertical frame

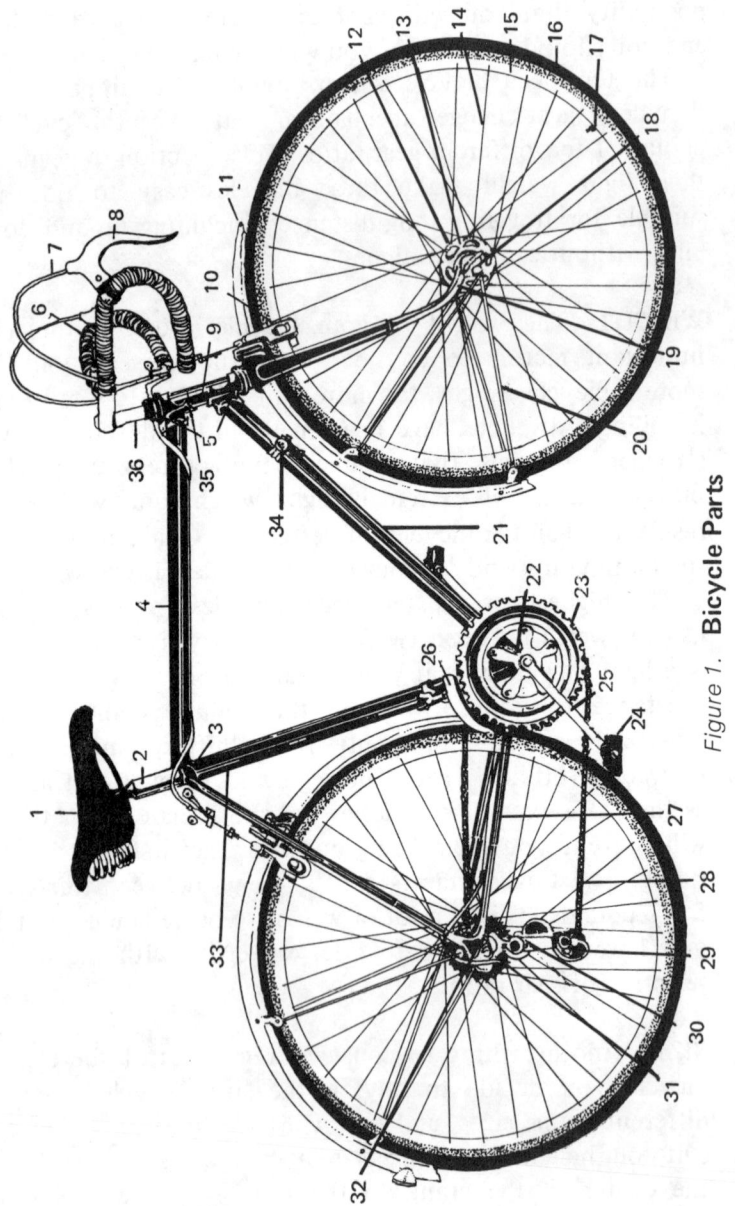

Figure 1. **Bicycle Parts**

1. Seat
2. Seat Post
3. Seat cluster lug
4. Top tube
5. Headset
6. Handlebars
7. Brake cable
8. Brake lever
9. Steering head
10. Caliper brake
11. Fender
12. High-flange hub
13. Wheel dropout
14. Spoke
15. Rim
16. Tire
17. Valve
18. Quick-release skewer
19. Fork
20. Fender brace
21. Down tube
22. Bottom bracket
23. Chainwheel
24. Pedal
25. Cotterless crank
26. Front derailleur
27. Chainstay
28. Chain
29. Tension roller for the rear derailleur
30. Rear derailleur
31. Freewheel gear cluster
32. Rear drop out
33. Seat tube
34. Gear-shift lever for rear derailleur
35. Lug
36. Handlebar stem

member. This measurement usually ranges from nineteen to twenty-seven inches. If the bicycle is the right size, you should be able to stand with both feet on the ground and just clear the horizontal frame member. This method of measurement may sound a bit crude, but it is the best way of fitting a bicycle to your height.

You should not confuse frame size with wheel size. Most bicycles have 26- or 27-inch wheels. The wheel size does not determine the frame size and vice versa. Make sure that you know what size frame you need and, when you purchase a bicycle, be sure to specify the frame size that you want.

GEAR SIZES: If you are going to buy an English racer, you will not have to worry about the selection of gear ratios. This choice has already been made for you and all the gears are hidden away in your rear hub. If you are considering a ten-speed, you will have to select the size of your gears. The size of the gears on your bicycle will determine what possibilities of gear ratio you will have to choose from while riding.

Sprocket size is determined by the number of teeth the sprocket has. The greater the number of teeth on a rear sprocket, the lower the gear that can be attained and the easier it is to pedal your bicycle. The smaller the sprocket, the higher the gear, and the harder it is to pedal. In selecting those sprockets you will want on your rear cluster, you should consider the range from the lowest to the highest gear. Generally speaking, a range that is not very wide will make the bicycle harder to ride than a wider range of gear ratios. The average cyclist should have a range on the rear cluster from 14 to 28 teeth and a front chain wheel with sprockets of 39 and 50 teeth. If you want a faster bicycle and are willing to develop the muscular ability needed to pedal it, you can select a smaller range, but be prepared to work a bit when climbing those hills.

QUALITY: The quality of a bicycle is determined by the quality of the parts used to make it. Different makes of bicycles are only different combinations of different bicycle components. To judge the quality of any particular bicycle, you will have to look at the manufacturer's list of components with some knowledge of what they all mean. The same bicycle could have a high-quality frame and a low-quality derailleur. Deciding which bicycle to buy will mean choosing those features which you want most in your price range. The better the quality of the components, and the greater the number of high-quality components, the better the quality of the bicycle and the higher the price. You should know which components and which features of a bicycle will make it a better machine.

FRAMES: The frame is one of the most important parts of a bicycle. It is the frame that gives the bicycle most of its weight, and in a low-quality frame this will be considerable. The frame is also important because it acts as the bicycle's suspension system. A high-quality frame will absorb most of the road shock that a low-quality frame would pass on to your body. The amount of road shock you experience has a direct bearing on the amount of fatigue you will feel. A strong, lightweight, resilient frame will be easier to pedal and less fatiguing than the heavier low-quality frames.

Most frames are made from seamed steel tubing. This tubing is a strip of steel that has been rolled into tubular shape and then welded. It is the variety usually found on English racers and is heavy as well as weak. The tubes are almost always fitted into one another and then welded at the joints. This weakens the frame because the temperature needed for welding affects the steel tubing adversely.

Better-quality bicycles will have seamless tubing that is made from steel alloys containing manganese molybdenum or chrome molybdenum. These alloys are lighter, stronger, and have greater resiliency than rolled steel. "Reynolds 531" is the best tubing available for bicycle frames.

One other aspect of frames that you should be aware of is the difference between straight gauge and double-butted tubing. Straight gauge tubing is the same thickness at all points along the tubes. Double-butted tubing is thickened at the ends for added strength. You will not be able to see the extra width since it is on the inside of the tube, so look for the word "double-butted" on the frame label.

You can usually recognize a high-quality frame by the manner in which the tubes are joined. The better-quality bicycles have lugs which the frame tubes are brazed into. This brazing requires lower temperatures than welding and therefore does not damage the metal and produces a stronger frame.

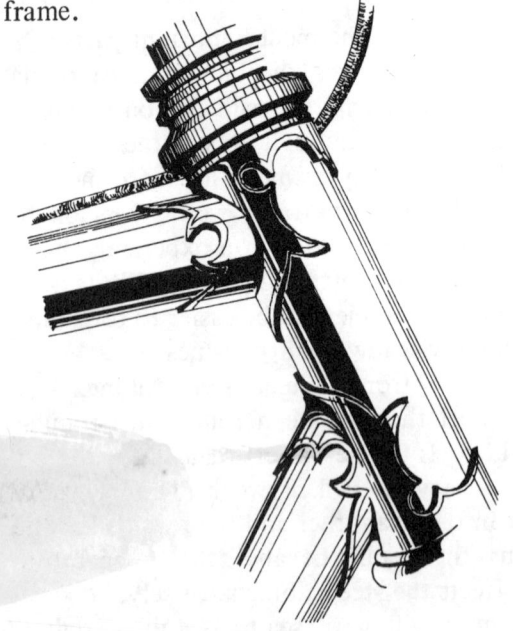

Figure 2.
**Frame Joints:
Lugged and Brazed**

I should mention something about the style of the frame

you select. Regardless of your sex, the so-called woman's bicycle should be avoided. These bicycle frames are not as well designed for strength and resiliency as the standard frames. In spite of their supposed benefits and practical value, they should not be purchased.

Forks are much the same as frames. All of the discussion applying to bicycle frames apply to forks as well. The best are made from steel alloys and are tubular. Nontubular forks are a sign of a low-quality bicycle.

CRANKS: There are three types of cranks currently in use: One-piece cranks are usually found on the less expensive American bicycles, whereas European bicycles use either cottered or cotterless cranks. Of the two European cranks the cotterless crank is better and more expensive. The cottered crank can be recognized by the pin which holds the crank in place. Cranks should be made of aluminum and not steel in higher quality bicycles.

Campagnolo cranks are the best, but they are extremely expensive. Stronglight, T.A., and Williams cranks are also of high quality.

PEDALS: There are three types of pedals: conventional rubber tread pedals, road racing pedals, and track racing pedals. The road racing and track racing pedals are the best to have if you are planning to do any touring with your bicycle.

Campagnolo pedals are the best. Another good pedal, which is also very durable and less expensive, is the Lyotard pedal.

DERAILLEURS: Campagnolo makes the best derailleurs (gear-changing mechanism). They are the quickest and easiest to shift and have the widest range of gears. They come in three grades, "Record," "Gran Sport," and "Sportsman." The Huret "Allvit" and Simplex "Prestige" are less expensive (and therefore more popular) high-quality derailleurs.

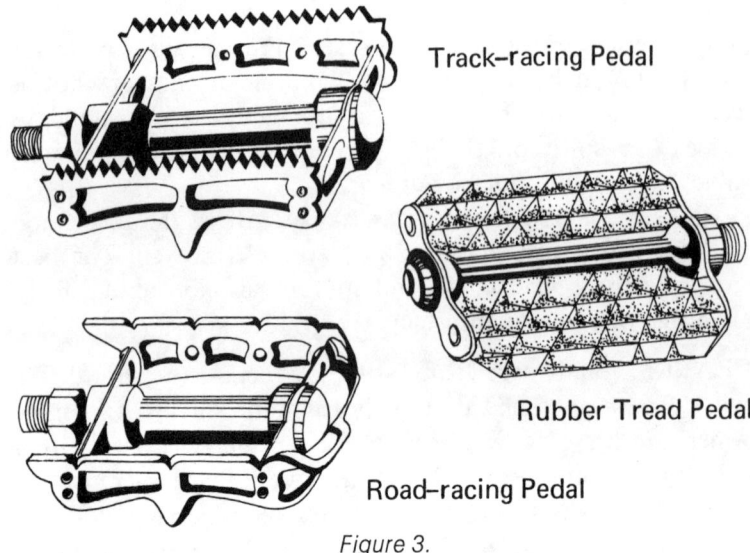

Figure 3.

CALIPER BRAKES: Caliper brakes are of two types—center-pull and side-pull. The center-pull caliper brakes are better because they operate with the brake cable, applying pressure to both brake caliper arms. On side-pull brakes, as the name implies, the cable is attached to the caliper-brake arms on one side and the pressure must be transferred to the other side of the rim along the pivot assembly. This causes uneven braking.

The best caliper brakes are made by Mafac. Mafac brakes have better adjustability than most other brakes on the market. Campagnolo and Weinmann are also high-quality brakes.

HUBS: Hubs should be of the one-piece, machined variety and not stamped metal. They come in two styles: conventional and quick release. The quick-release hubs enable you to remove your wheels without the use of tools and are found on more expensive bicycles. The best hubs are made by Campagnolo. Normandy, Simplex, and Cinelli hubs are also of high quality.

RIMS: Rims are made for either clincher or sew-up tires. Your choice of rims will depend on the type of tire you want to ride on. The clincher tires are more durable, but they also weigh more and are harder to pedal than sew-ups.

The best rims are made from lightweight aluminum alloys. Steel rims are a sign of lower quality. Mavic, Fiamme, and Weinmann are all good-quality rims.

SADDLE: Saddles come in three styles: the spring type, the touring saddle, and the racing saddle. You should have either the touring or racing saddle if you are buying a good-quality bicycle since these are better suited to the proper pedaling position that you will be using. The best saddle is made by Brooks.

HANDLEBARS: The more expensive bicycles all have turned-down or flat handlebars. The raised handlebars found on lower-quality bicycles do not enable a rider to assume the proper pedaling position, making it harder for him to pedal the bicycle.

WHERE TO BUY A BICYCLE: You should never buy a bicycle from any place that does not deliver it assembled free of charge. This eliminates all discount and department stores, and for good reasons. They do not usually have the personnel that are trained in bicycle repair or assembly, and you are liable to end up assembling the bicycle yourself or having it arrive assembled improperly. You will also have difficulty if there should be any repairs needed once you get your bicycle. If something should go wrong after you get your bike, the best most chain stores can do is send it back to the manufacturer or try to get you to exchange it for another one. If you buy your bicycle from a place staffed by personnel who know their way around bicycles, you will get your new bicycle assembled properly and have somewhere to take it when you have problems that need to be ironed out.

Chapter 3

Accessories

Accessories are an important part of bicycling. They make it possible to use one basic bicycle for a variety of different purposes. One day your bicycle may be a featherweight, ready to scale the highest of hills; the next day it is something more akin to a packhorse. With the right accessories, you can go from a machine equipped only for a lighthearted jog around the neighborhood to a complete camping vehicle which will carry you and your equipment far afield. Some accessories are useful to all bicycle owners and others are only designed for cyclists with more specialized interests. Just which accessories you will want or need will depend to some extent upon the type of bicycling that you intend to do.

Regardless of which accessories you choose to buy, one fact should always be taken into consideration: any accessories that you decide upon will add a certain amount of weight to your bicycle. The more your bicycle weighs, the more work you will have to do to get it rolling and keep it rolling. Some of the more welcome advances in recent bicycle technology have been made in the development of stronger materials that enable manufacturers to produce lighter bicycles. The modern bicycle is more responsive, faster, and easier to pedal than its cumbersome predecessors. If your bicycle is loaded down with many unnecessary extras, you will only succeed in nullifying the years of important research it has taken to produce the freewheeling machines of today.

LIGHTS: Though lights are occasionally useful when picking your way through the country on dark nights, they are designed mainly to be seen by others. In most states it is required by law to have both front and rear lights on when riding at night, so that the cyclist will be visible to the passing motorists who, otherwise, may have a hard time seeing a bicyclist in front of them.

Battery-operated lights are heavy, unreliable, and contain parts that must be constantly replaced. The cheaper ones have faulty connections; the more expensive types, which have better wiring, are heavier and need heavier mountings. Since these lights need batteries, and batteries have a habit of dying, it is advisable to carry spares in case of failure. A spare bulb is also needed since the bulbs do not last long with the jostling they receive while riding. Another problem of most battery-operated lights is that they invariably rattle. This may not sound like a serious problem, but it can quickly put a damper on those quiet rides through the country.

Dynamo lights have a small generator which mounts on either the rear wheel or the front hub and turns with the motion of the bicycle to produce electricity. These lights are generally lighter and less prone to failure than battery-operated lights. However, they only produce light when the bicycle is in motion. If you have to slow down the light will become weak, and stopping turns it off completely. This is a major drawback if you have to stop for repairs on a dark night. Some dynamo lights can also be run on batteries in case of generator failure or for use when the bicycle is not in motion.

One other problem created by the use of dynamo lights is the drag which they produce on the wheel. With the improved generators of today, however, the drag has been reduced considerably and will probably pass unnoticed by any other than those with the most tender of sensibilities. Dynamos are more expensive than the battery-operated lights (the dynamo assemblies cost between $5.00 and $10.00), but their light weight and greater reliability make them worth the extra investment.

There is a small French light that straps to the arm or leg and runs on batteries which can be purchased for $1.75. It is lightweight and has a white light forward and a red light to the rear. If strapped to the leg it will also have an up and down motion, making it all the more visible to passing motorists. It is easily removed for use when making repairs or reading maps at night. You may have some trouble with the straps on this light since they are not very durable. The bulbs also have a very short lifespan, making this light more suitable for part-time use or for use as a spare. Its easy accessability and high visibility are useful if you are going to go on a long trip.

HORNS: Horns come in a variety of sizes and with a variety of sound potentials. For the most part they are not particularly helpful in situations when you would be most likely to use them. It is better to rely on your own ability to maneuver out of a dangerous situation than on someone else's ability to recognize your warning. In most emergencies it is safer to have both hands on the handlebars, where they can control the bicycle, than to be fumbling with a horn. If noise is necessary, your increased lung power should give you the shouting ability needed to produce it.

Freon-powered boat horns are available that will produce a blast worthy of more than just notice for a price that won't go unnoticed either. They cost approximately $7.00, and refills will run $1.75 each. They are good for frightening the stoutest of motorists into making a sudden dash for cover. If he happens to dash in the right direction you are safe, provided of course that he doesn't have a quick temper and an impulse for revenge. Such frightening power can cause more accidents than it prevents.

Battery-operated electric horns offer a more reasonable sound potential, but, like the battery-operated lights, they are not very reliable. They are capable of producing an annoying amount of rattle, batteries have to be replaced periodically, and they add a substantial amount of weight to a bicycle. The $1.50 to $2.50 that you spend for these horns will more than likely be a waste of money.

Bulb horns are probably the most practical noisemakers available. They are simply designed and there is, therefore, less that can go wrong. The rubber bulbs will have a tendency to wear out or come loose from the cone, making them not altogether trouble free, but compared to the alternatives, this is a minor consideration. They can be quite heavy so a smaller one would probably be adequate and more practical to use than the larger ones. Prices range from $1.95 to $3.95.

The bell or tinkle horns are inexpensive (as low as $.49) and much lighter than any of the other horns. They do not last very long, however, and their ability to be heard is rather questionable. They would not be very effective against motorists and they are not likely to be heard above the noise of traffic, but they do work well in warning pedestrians of your approach.

BAGS AND PANNIERS: It is advisable to have at least one bag, such as a saddle bag, in which you can carry tools, spare parts, maps, and a cycle cape, regardless of the amount of cycling you intend to do. Even if you only intend to ride around your own neighborhood, it is better not to get caught on the road without the proper equipment. For tours or camping trips with your bicycle, you will need panniers to carry the extra articles needed to ensure safe and comfortable cycling over extended periods of time.

The bags or panniers that you select should be as strong and as lightweight as possible. This usually means spending a bit more for them, but the problems you will save will more than make up for the extra cost. Straps should be especially durable since they suffer the greatest amount of wear and tear. There is nothing more infuriating than problems while on the road because of something as simple as a broken strap. Plastic should generally be avoided, leather being much more reliable and worth the extra investment. Some of the synthetic materials, such as nylon and rayon, though not as reliable as leather are, for the most part, adequate and usually weigh less. Try to get a bag or set of panniers which will have many small pockets for easy access to frequently used items and greater ease in distributing the weight of your gear evenly on the bicycle. Make sure that the bag or pannier you select is waterproof. Even if you don't plan on riding in the rain, a waterproof bag is necessary for those times when you get caught in a downpour.

Bags range in price from $1.95 to upwards of $10.00 and can be mounted behind the seat or on the handlebars. Panniers can be mounted astride either the front or rear wheel and cost from $12.00 to $30.00 depending on the quality. If you are packing for a trip you should try to distribute the weight of your gear as evenly as possible, making it wise to have both front and rear pannier bags. This may run into a bit of money but it will make the bicycle much easier to handle and ride much more smoothly—important if you are going to ride any appreciable distance.

You should never mount a bag on the middle part of your bicycle. This will cause no small number of problems in trying to keep from dislodging it while riding. It is also not advisable to ride with a pack on your back. The bicycle is perfectly capable of carrying the burden and with any weight on your back you will only succeed in making yourself tired and uncomfortable within a very short period of time.

Bags and panniers should be mounted with supports. This ensures a sturdy fit and makes the possibility of damage to your bicycle from faulty mounting negligible. Supports will also keep your bags from coming apart at the seams. Supports should be lightweight, sturdy, and made to fit your bicycle. Don't risk possible damage by trying to fit the wrong support onto your bicycle.

BASKETS: Baskets are easier to carry items in if you are only going a short distance and want to be able to load and unload your bicycle with ease. They are ideal for grocery shopping or running errands around your own neighborhood. Metal baskets are noisy and expensive, but plastic and woven varieties are also available. Baskets are a handy accessory to have if you plan to use your bicycle mainly for transportation within your own neighborhood.

BABY CARRIERS: If you have a small child and are planning to take it with you while riding, you should have a carrier made for that purpose. The carrier should mount over the rear wheel. The front wheel should be free to steer and the added weight of even a small child will make the bicycle hard to control. Make sure that the carrier has a strap to hold the child in place and a foot support to keep his feet from dangling in the spokes.

MUDGUARDS: Anyone, with the exception of a few of the heartier enthusiasts, who has ever been caught in the rain without mudguards can testify to the advantages of having them on your bicycle. Mudguards keep water and mud from spinning off the wheel and onto the rider. The plastic ones are best, being lighter and quieter than metal. If you already have metal mudguards on your bicycle it would be worth the $5.00 investment to exchange them for plastic ones.

BOTTLES AND CARRIERS: Cycling can be a thirsty business. On a hot day water is an essential part of the cyclist's equipment. No rider should be without a water bottle if he intends to be out on the road for more than a couple of hours. Water bottles can be kept in carriers mounted on the handlebars or on the down-cross tube. Hip flasks are also available which can be carried in a spare pocket, but it is much easier and less cumbersome to have a bottle mounted on the bicycle. Bottles and flasks come in either lightweight aluminum or plastic; and sell for from $1.00 to $2.00. Carriers sell for approximately $2.00.

ODOMETERS AND SPEEDOMETERS: It is often useful to see how far you have ridden on your bicycle, but there is rarely any need to know how fast you are traveling at any particular point in time. The important thing to a cyclist is his overall or average speed; therefore speedometers are a waste of money. They will only add extra weight and produce a sizable amount of drag on the wheel.

Odometers, although they have a greater practical value than speedometers, are noisy (they make a clicking sound when hitting the spokes) and, not being made to operate at higher speeds, they tend to jam up on downhill runs. This can cause considerable damage to your spokes. They are also difficult to install and will invariably fall out of place when the front wheel is removed. If you want to know how far you have gone, it is much better to use a map and dipense with the gadgetry. If you do get an odometer, make sure that you get one that fits your wheel size.

COMPASSES: Unless you plan to ride your bicycle through uncharted territory, in which case you would need constant reference to a compass, a small pocket compass will more than adequately serve your needs. The kind that mounts on your handlebars and floats in a northerly direction may look sophisticated, but it is an expensive and unnecessary appendage.

KICKSTANDS: More accurately described as "pushovers," kickstands are heavy, weighing up to a pound, and must be bolted on, which means that they can become unbolted. Aside from the added weight, kickstands rarely do what they are supposed to do. They are not very steady and impossible to use where there is soft ground. It is much safer to lean your bicycle against something that won't fall over. If you must have a kickstand, get one with an adjustable leg.

TIRE PUMPS: To protect your tires from damage they should be kept at the proper inflation. With tubular tires, this means that they must be inflated regularly. The tubular tires have very thin walls which allow air to pass from the tire constantly. Tires that are underinflated will wear out fast and make it harder to pedal your bicycle. To keep your tires at the proper inflation, you should have a tire pump. Pumps are also necessary for fixing flat tires while on the road, and anyone who rides a bicycle will have to do just that sooner or later.

The hand pumps which can be mounted on the bicycle are the best investment. Zefal is a good brand name and their pumps sell for from $1.50 to $2.25. Be sure to get a pump-to-valve connector which fits your valve since they come in different sizes.

TUBE-REPAIR KIT: A repair kit is a must if you are going to ride on tires, which, all things considered, is a good idea. Dunlop is probably the best. Their tube repair kit (for use with clincher tires) sells for $.60 and the kit for tubulars sells for $1.60. The tubular repair kit could use more needles and thread, so it might be a good idea to purchase these when you buy the kit. If you do ride on tubulars, make sure you get a kit that contains ultrathin patches. Thick patches will leave a bulge in the tire after the repair is made and this bulge will cause a thumping sound as you ride.

AIR PRESSURE GAUGE: Since accurate pressure is important to your tires, you should have a pressure gauge. The gauge will help to prevent blowouts caused by overinflated tires. You should get a good-quality gauge because the cheap ones are usually inaccurate. The gauge should read to at least 120 pounds per square inch.

NAILPULLERS: Nailpullers are a light and inexpensive protection for your tires. They are mounted on the brakes or forks so that they barely ride on the tire while it is turning. If the tire should pick up any broken glass, rocks, nails, etc., the nailpuller will remove them before they have a chance to become imbedded and cause damage to the tire or puncture the tube.

PEDAL PARAPHERNALIA: In order to get the most enjoyment possible from your bicycle, you will have to pedal

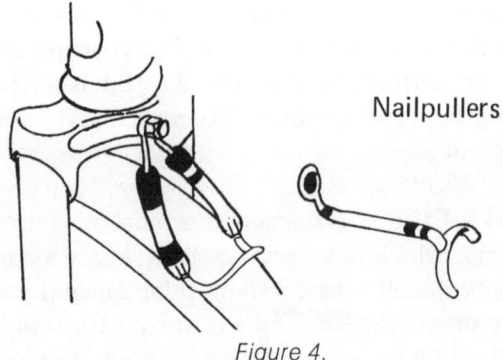

Figure 4.

properly. This means learning how to "ankle." In order to ankle properly, you will need the accessories to keep your feet securely placed on the pedals.

Toe clips provide a 40 to 50 percent increase in your cycling efficiency. They enable the cyclist to pull up on the pedals as well as push down and are an absolute must for touring or racing. They come in different sizes so you have to purchase a pair that fit properly or you will end up with sore feet. The $1.50 you spend on a pair of toe clips will have a marked effect on your ability to pedal.

Rattrap pedals and shoes with cleats attached to the soles are also a big help in keeping your feet secure. The shoes should have soft tops for comfort and hard soles for a minimum of foot fatigue. Cleats can be fastened to your shoes at any shoe repair shop, but you should make sure that they are placed in the proper position. Your foot should rest on the pedal in the same position it would normally be without the cleats. When you buy the shoes, ride with them for a while before putting the cleats on. This will give you a good idea of about where your foot meets the pedal. If you don't want to spend the money to buy special riding shoes, you should ride with a soft leather shoe. Tennis shoes should not be worn while riding. They will give you sore feet and a poor response from your bicycle.

Having your feet firmly attached to the pedals will also help to prevent accidents. It is not uncommon for a cyclist with improper footgear to slide off the pedals and onto the pavement.

CLOTHING: Clothing should always be lightweight and suited to the weather in which you intend to ride. On some days the temperature can vary considerably so it is a good idea to have both cool and warm clothing along if you intend to be gone for the entire day.

Jerseys should be made of double-knit wool or cotton and preferably have lots of pockets. Pockets always come in handy for carrying small articles that may be useful while riding. Shorts are usually made of wool, and some of them come with padding, a good idea for anyone who rides enough to get saddle sore. Gloves should be made with thick palms and lightweight backs. Gloves keep your hands from getting sore and also help you establish a firm grip on the handlebars. In addition, should you take a spill it is likely that you will scrape your hands on the pavement. Gloves will help you keep your skin intact. If you do any cycling in cold weather it is also a good idea to have a pair of woolen mittens to keep your hands warm while riding.

Crash helmets are a good safety precaution. They reduce the possibility of serious injury in case you should have an accident. It is always better to be safe, and bicycle crash helmets do not restrict vision or freedom of movement to any appreciable extent.

A rain cape is a necessity. Even if you don't plan on riding in the rain, you will still need one for those times when you didn't plan on it. Nature is still unpredictable and weather can change with very little warning so be prepared and it won't matter. Plastic capes are too warm and they rip easily so you should try to find one made from rip stop material. It will last longer and be much more comfortable.

HANDLEBAR GRIPS: Handlebar grips are a waste of money and will cause more problems than they solve. Plastic does not breathe, and your hands will sweat causing much discomfort and the possibility of a slippery hold on your bicycle. You are much better off taping your handlebars. Tape will give you a firmer grip and allow you to take a variety of hand positions, an important luxury on long rides.

BIKE COVERS: A bike cover will help you to keep your bicycle safe from the effects of adverse weather. If you intend to keep your bicycle outside when it isn't in use, a cover is a must. Water can quickly corrode and ruin many bicycle parts if they are not protected. A bicycle cover will help to keep your bicycle dry. Get a cover that fits your bicycle, one that doesn't will be a constant problem. You should also get one that is lightweight for easier carrying.

TRAINING ROLLERS: If you plan to use your bicycle for keeping in shape or if you want to keep in shape for using your bicycle, training rollers are great. They enable you to keep up your cycling through the worst of seasonal weather. They come with a stand and rollers which allow you to pedal for miles without leaving your house. For anyone who lives in colder climates, these machines are ideal for staying in shape through the long and cold winter months.

TOOLS: To keep your bicycle running properly you will have to service it regularly and, to make this easier, you should invest in the proper tools. Your tools will enable you to make repairs, both at home and on the road, which will more than make up for their cost by saving you the outlandish fees currently charged by bicycle repair shops. It is possible in some cases to use conventional tools, but if you have a foreign-made bicycle or a bicycle that has foreign parts, it will have metric and Allen nuts, bolts, and screws. These will require special tools.

ACCESSORIES

A Mafac tool kit, that can be purchased for $3.00, contains spanners and wrenches that will fit most of the small metric parts on your bicycle. It will also fit derailleur parts on all except Campagnolo derailleurs. This kit is a necessity for the cyclist who intends to do any touring with his bicycle. Repairs often must be made when the cyclist is far from home, and this tool kit can be carried easily.

A metric Allen-wrench set contains tools that will fit almost any bicycle parts using Allen nuts and screws. This set can be purchased for under $1.00 and will prove an invaluable aid if your bicycle has foreign parts.

If you have a derailleur you will need a chain riveter-extractor. There will be no master link on your chain because the extra size of the link would not fit through the derailleur gear-changing mechanism. For $1.75 you can get this small tool that will remove and replace the rivets in your chain when you have to remove it for servicing.

To remove pedal bearings and clean them you should have a wing-nut pedal wrench. This only costs about $.60 and will save you time and trouble when cleaning your pedal bearings.

To adjust the cones on your wheels you can use a pair of pliers or an adjustable wrench, but there is a tool that is especially made for this job. Hub offset wrenches cost about $3.95 a set so you may want to do without, but if you can afford them it will save time and trouble as well as reduce the possibility of damage to the adjusting cones.

To service your crank bearings you should have a C-spanner. This tool fits the locknut on the bottom bracket of the bicycle and will make the removal of your crank bearings easier.

To keep your rims from going out of round you will have to check your spokes regularly. To tighten or replace spokes you should purchase a spoke wrench. They only cost about $.35 and will help to keep your wheels aligned and rolling properly.

There is a variety of other tools at various prices, but the ones mentioned above will do practically everything that you will need to do to keep your bicycle in good running condition. If you are reluctant to buy tools after spending a lot of money on your bicycle in the first place, remember that the extra investment will keep your expensive bicycle looking and running like an expensive bicycle.

Chapter 4

Learning to Ride

There is more to learning to ride a bicycle than might be expected. If you have ever seen a bicycle race, you may have noticed that each rider had a highly stylized form for obtaining the greatest possible speed and efficiency with the muscles at his disposal. Riding a modern bicycle means more than just learning to steer straight while turning the pedals. This may be a good place to start if you have never ridden a bicycle before, but it is only a start. It should by no means be satisfactory for anyone who wishes to get the greatest possible enjoyment from his bicycle.

BEGINNERS: Even if you have never been on a bicycle before in your life, it should only take a few hours to master the basic principles of balance. The forward motion of a two-wheeler gives it a great deal of stability once you get going. You can prove this by giving your bicycle a good push while riderless (make sure you run along beside it). The bicycle will balance itself as long as there is sufficient forward motion. The trick to learning how to ride a bicycle lies in keeping your balance long enough to attain this forward motion.

The other factor which has a direct influence on the stability of a bicycle is the steering movement of the front wheel. If the bicycle should start to tilt to one side, you need only to give the handlebars a slight twist in that direction to regain your balance. This response seems to come naturally to most people and very few actually have to learn it.

If you are just learning to ride, it is best to do so with a bicycle that is closer to the ground than the one that you will eventually end up riding. Whatever you do, don't start with a bicycle that is too tall. It is hard for a person who can already ride to manage a bicycle that is too big, let alone someone who is trying to learn to balance.

You should adjust the seat on your bicycle so that your feet can rest on the ground when you are sitting on the saddle. This will give you the confidence of knowing that you can catch yourself if you should start to lose your balance. After making sure that you know where the brakes are, start at the top of a good incline (pick a road that has no traffic) and push along the ground with your feet to get the bicycle rolling. It is better not to worry about pedaling until you have gotten the feel of how a bicycle balances. It is much harder to maintain your balance while pedaling than when you are just coasting. When it feels safe to do so, you should put your feet on the pedals and just let gravity supply the forward motion necessary to stay on the bicycle. After trying this a few times you should have a pretty good idea of how to maintain your balance.

Once you can balance a bicycle successfully, you should again place yourself at the top of the hill. This time, when you place your feet on the pedals, turn them slowly. You will begin to feel how to keep your balance while the crank is turning. As you feel more confident you can apply more effort to the pedals and soon you will not need the incline of the hill to maintain your forward motion.

Once you have mastered the problems of balance and pedaling you should practice turning and stopping on a bicycle. When turning and stopping come naturally to you, you should practice hand signals. It is not as easy to keep your balance while one hand is signaling, but it will not take long to master this necessary feat of coordination. A cyclist should not go out into traffic until he feels confident and can make all the necessary maneuvers while riding that he will need when on the road.

BODY POSITION: The position of the cyclist's body is very important. It may not seem crucial at first, but if you are to use your body in the most efficient manner possible, it has to be in the best possible position.

If you sit erect on a bicycle, most of your weight will be carried on the seat. This leaves your legs and feet with all the work. Try sitting up straight and pedaling to see how it feels. Your legs will feel quite powerless and will fatigue rapidly.

If you sit too far forward, your weight will be resting mostly on your hands and feet. This will cause fatigue more rapidly than if you assume the correct position. Not only will you lose efficiency, you will also lose the ability to supply that extra little burst of power needed to send you over the crest of an approaching hill.

To obtain the most efficient use of the muscles in your body your weight should be evenly distributed between the three points of contact with the bicycle: the seat, the handlebars, and the pedals. To accomplish this your body should lean slightly forward until you feel evenly supported at all three points of contact. In this position you will be able to use the muscles of your arms, legs, feet, ankles, back, and abdomen to drive the pedals.

Keep your knees in a direct line with the line of your bicycle. You should never pedal by throwing your knees wide to the right or left when turning the pedals. You should keep your knees in as close to the bicycle as possible to achieve the greatest amount of power transfer from your body to the pedals. Remember that a good, smooth, and consistent motion of the legs will give you far more response for your effort than jerky, unbalanced movements.

ANKLING: It is not uncommon to see people riding their bicycles by shifting their weight from one pedal to the other. Many people do not know that proper cycling does not depend upon gravity alone. By applying weight to the pedal once it has reached the top of its revolution and letting up on it once it reaches the bottom, you are really only driving the pedal through 120 degrees of its 360-degree revolution. During the other 2/3 of the pedal's orbit there is no power being supplied to the pedal, ·it having been transferred entirely to the other side. Aside from being extremely inefficient, this method of cycling also produces a very spasmodic ride. The jerky action of the pedals, something akin to a couple of pistons, and the side-to-side pull caused by the shifting of the body weight make it impossible to ride smoothly or in a straight line. The body will soon become fatigued and the ride will be more of a jostling than a relaxing jaunt.

The crank on your bicycle supplies power to the rear wheel by moving in a circle. To obtain the greatest amount of drive your pressure on the pedals should also be circular. The up and down motion does not keep the sprocket rotating smoothly and creates uneven tension on the chain. If you have ever turned a crank by hand, you will have some idea what this circular motion feels like.

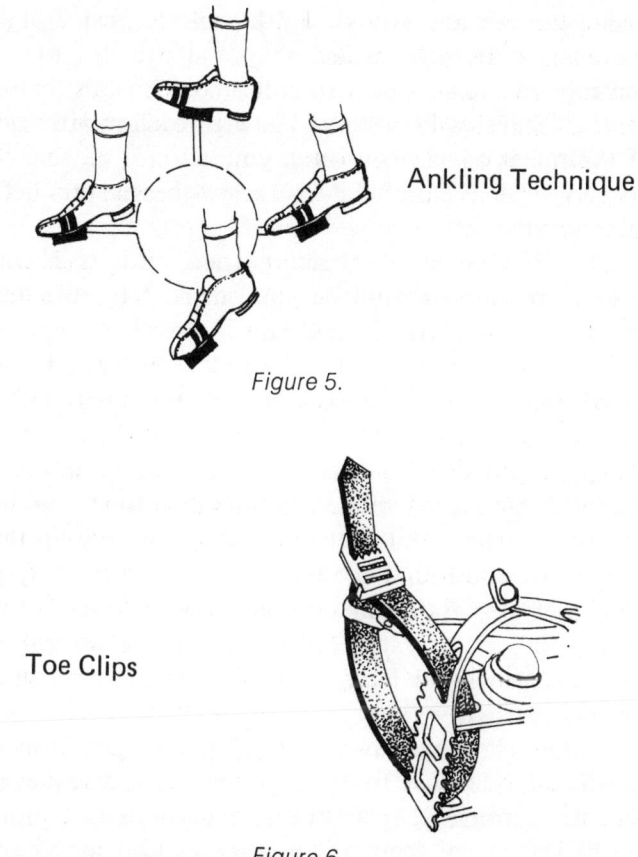

Ankling Technique

Figure 5.

Toe Clips

Figure 6.

When the pedals are in the vertical position, at the top and bottom of the turn, both feet should be exerting a slight amount of pressure on the pedals. This will carry the pedals through the vertical position and start the downward and upward portion of the turn smoothly. The ankles must be used to exert this pressure and keep a smooth spinning motion to the pedals.

When either foot approaches the top pedal position, the ankle should be flexed upward. Your heel should be lower than your toe and you should be able to push from behind the pedal somewhat to get it up and over the top position and into the downstroke. In order to do this, the ball of your foot will have to be used. If you are pedaling with the arches of your feet or with the toes, you will not be able to ankle properly and will probably end up with sore feet before the ride is over.

Once the pedal has been pushed into its downstroke, weight and drive should be applied. At the same time your ankle should extend gradually, exerting pressure and straightening the foot. When the pedal is halfway through the downstroke (at the 3 o'clock position), your foot should be almost horizontal.

As the pedal approaches the 6 o'clock position the foot should extend even further. This will enable you to apply pressure to the pedal with your ankle and sweep the pedal back when you round the bottom of the stroke. By pushing back with this foot and pushing forward with the opposite foot, you will carry the crank through the vertical position with a motion that is an extension, not an interruption, of the pedal stroke.

Ankling may seem awkward at first, but give your muscles a chance to get used to it and you will find that it eventually becomes automatic. It will be as much a part of your ride as the bicycle itself. You will quickly realize that your ride is much smoother and your body less prone to fatigue.

TOE CLIPS: With proper ankling, you can push the pedal through approximately 240 degrees, or 2/3 of its 360-degree revolution. You have already doubled your efficiency! To increase your efficiency even further you should learn what every racing cyclist knows and depends on for maximum speed and minimum effort.

LEARNING TO RIDE

Toe clips enable you not only to ankle on the downstroke, but on the upstroke as well. As your foot passes the 7 o'clock position you have no grip on the pedals unless your foot is fastened to them with toe clips. If you have a grip on the pedal, you can exert an upward pull as the pedal moves toward the top of the stroke.

As you pull up on the pedal your ankle should be bending in preparation for pushing it through the 12 o'clock position. Thus your ankle is supplying constant pressure to the pedals by contracting and expanding throughout the turn of the crank. With your ankles and legs supplying power through the complete cycle, you have increased your efficiency another 30 percent.

With toe clips and proper ankling you will have smooth, circular pedaling power. Once the spin becomes natural you will be able to pedal for long distances at respectable speeds, without excess fatigue.

HILLS: Hills are always a challenge to the cyclist. Some cyclists pride themselves on their ability to climb the steepest of them. Cycling over mountain passes is more popular than one would imagine after facing a few of the grades in his own neighborhood. It is a true test of a cyclist's stamina and cycling ability.

Though you may not be as happy to see a hill aproaching as a high-altitude cyclist, there is a good method for scaling your Everests without using up all of your energy. If you do not have multiple gears of some kind on your bicycle, no method is going to keep you from struggling on hills, but a gear selection and the proper technique can cut most grades down to size.

When you approach a hill, the immediate temptation is to rise up off the seat and start pumping for all you are worth. You should resist this temptation and keep a good steady pedaling rhythm. You should gradually lean your body forward and pull up slightly on the handlebars. This will force more of your body weight into the pedals and increase your power. As you start to slow down, you will have to change to a lower gear with a quick, sure movement.

Gears were made for conquering hills. With a derailleur gear changer, you have a wide range of gear ratios to choose from to enable you to maintain a constant pedal speed through a wide range of topographies. You should learn to estimate which gear on your bicycle will take you over the top of any hill that you approach without having drastically to increase your output of energy.

You should shift gears while you still have good speed. Do not wait until you have slowed to a standstill before changing into a lower gear. With derailleurs you will have to have considerable speed left to be able to get your chain on a lower gear sprocket.

By shifting early enough to a lower gear, you will be able to keep the same smooth spin on your pedals from a level surface to the top of a hill and over. Once you have reached the top and start to descend, you can shift back into a higher gear and continue your ride with only the slightest hint of interruption. Remember that the best method of cycling is a consistent, rythmical spin of the pedals, regardless of the terrain.

Chapter 5

Getting in Shape

It is easy and fun to bicycle your way toward physical fitness. However, as in any sport or fitness program, it will take some mental as well as physical work. A good program for increasing your muscular ability, lung power, and endurance should be planned in advance. Without proper planning your efforts will, at best, be in vain and in some cases even harmful. Many people have done real damage to their bodies while attempting to improve them. Physical exertion is beneficial only if conducted properly.

PREPARATION: In order to effectively improve your physical condition it is necessary to know what your condition is at present. If you are under thirty years of age you will not have to worry much about whether or not you are ready to start a cycling program. Unless there is evidence of heart ailment, in which case all physical activity should be monitored by your doctor, you can start right away with little cause for worry. You should still start slowly. Trying to do too much too fast will lead to more sore muscles and much less follow-through than if you follow a well-planned schedule of cycling. Do not try to set records your first week out. It does the body very little good to exercise in short bursts. Only a steady, sustained effort will produce sound health.

For those people over thirty, more care should be taken when starting a cycling exercise program. Those who are already physically active will probably be in good enough condition and will progress at a fast rate, but there will still be a period of time needed for the body to accustom itself to a new activity. People who lead inactive lives should start easy on a program of physical fitness.

Anyone who is not active or is not sure exactly what their physical condition is should have a physical examination before starting on an exercise program. An electrocardiogram should be included in the examination. Most of the serious injury caused by overexertion has occurred in people who have some form of heart ailment. Heart ailments should not necessarily stop a person from exercising, but care should be taken to avoid harm. Someone trained in medicine should oversee the activities of a person with any kind of heart difficulty.

Once you are sure that it is safe to exercise, you should plan a program that will take from ten to sixteen weeks and will have a definite goal to be reached within that period of time. A longer time will be needed for those with medical problems. There are two factors to consider when planning your prospective course toward fitness—distance and speed. Both distance and speed bear a direct relationship to the amount of exercise you will be getting. The greater the distance, the more activity it will take to cover it. The faster the time in covering a given distance, the greater the amount of physical activity required. These two factors should be varied to increase your physical output each week. They should also vary from day to day. One day you can cover a greater distance at a slower speed and the next day a shorter distance at a higher speed. This will give your program some variety, making it more enjoyable and much easier to stick to.

WARM-UP: The warm-up is as important as proper preparation. It is actually nothing more than daily preparation. Just as you can get very little benefit, and even possible harm, from trying to become physically fit your first couple of days out on the road, you can also do harm by trying to set records your first few minutes out during the day. You should start your ride easy, giving your body a chance to loosen up. A few minutes of stretching exercises before you even mount your bicycle would also help. Take a nice easy pedaling pace for the first few miles. Then you can increase your speed and start to exercise. Pulled muscles and torn ligaments can be caused by trying to do too much too fast. If your body is stiff when you start to exert it, it will be more than stiff afterwards. Again it should be emphasized that exercise should start slow and easy—then go all out. Push your body as much as you can, for that is what is beneficial about exercise, but not until your body is ready for it.

EXERCISE: The major portion of your daily run should consist of alternating periods of exertion and easing off during the first week or two. If your muscles start to feel really tired, you should dismount and walk for a few minutes. Don't sit down or stop moving entirely, but walk until your body recovers and you feel your muscles relax. Then mount your bicycle again and continue exercising.

With the proper preparation and warm-up out of the way,

you should set a good steady cycling pace and keep it up. You should be able to feel the strain on your muscles and respiratory system after you have been cycling for awhile. You will have to push yourself a bit if you expect to increase your strength and endurance, so don't hold back. Give yourself a good workout and before long you will find that you can increase your speed and your distance without feeling strained.

Towards the end of your ride you should go all out. Increase your spin as much as possible and hold it steady until you feel you cannot hold it any longer. You must exert yourself beyond what you are used to if your body is going to progress at all. Some exertion is better than none, but if you want your health improved and your stamina increased, you will have to sustain some real exertion every day.

You should feel healthily fatigued after exercise, but never abnormally tired. If you feel sluggish and extremely sore the next day, you are trying to do too much too fast. Slow down and let your body become accustomed to the exertion gradually. There is bound to be some soreness in your muscles, especially when you first start out, but if there is extreme soreness and you have trouble moving the next day, you are trying to go too fast.

Unless you discover that your schedule is too demanding, in which case it should be altered to fit your personal capacities better, stick to the course you have outlined. A regular plan of activity will ensure you regular and beneficial exercise. There will be some days when you feel you can do more than you originally planned. If this happens you should go ahead and do it. If it happens regularly, there is something wrong with your schedule.

COOLING DOWN: Just as important as a good warm-up before physical exertion, is a good cooling-down period after. Five to ten minutes of cooling down is needed to prevent

GETTING IN SHAPE

your body from being subjected to extremes of activity before it is able to adjust. The last five to ten minutes of riding should be easy and designed to let your muscles gradually relax after the strain you have put them through. Pedaling as hard as you can for home and then flopping down in an easy chair can cause cramping, dizziness, and sometimes even fainting. Your body has to unwind slowly and should be given plenty of time to make the adjustment from activity to inactivity. If you should find yourself in a position where you have to stop abruptly in the middle of your cycling, such as to repair a flat tire, it is better to set your bicycle down for a few minutes and walk around until you catch your breath and your muscles have a chance to unwind than to sit down immediately to make the repair.

You should also avoid sudden changes of temperature after exercise. Taking your windbreaker off after working up a sweat can cool your body too quickly. While you are exercising, your blood is concentrated in the areas of muscle which you use and this limits the ability of the body to deal with rapid changes in temperature. Your blood has to have a chance to redistribute itself evenly throughout your body before it experiences any sudden change in temperature.

Cycling may be thirsty work on a hot day, but you should let your body cool down before you rush to the water fountain to quench your thirst. Cold water should be taken in small quantities after a hard workout. Gulping down water may satisfy your thirst, but it may also cause stomach cramps. If you have a water bottle on your bicycle, you won't have to worry because you can replace the water that your body loses during the ride.

BEST TIME OF DAY: It is obvious that you should try to avoid those times when there will be a great deal of traffic on the roads, but beyond that consideration, any time is fine for exercise. Whether you get up early and ride a few miles before starting your daily routine, or ride a few miles after the day is over makes no difference to your body. Some people find it hard to get moving in the morning and would probably be better off if they didn't ride while half asleep and low on energy. Other people would be better off getting a good vigorous workout in the early morning hours to prepare themselves for the day's activities.

Regardless of what time of day you choose for your cycling program, it should take place at the same time every day. Choose a time that is convenient. You shouldn't try to squeeze it in so that you will have an excuse for skipping a day of cycling. Only through a continuous program can you hope to increase your capacity for cycling and keep your body healthy. Allow plenty of time and, once the routine is down, you will find that it really doesn't take that much out of your day. The time you spend on good exercise will be more than made up for by the increase in energy and alertness you will gain.

WEEKEND CYCLIST: If your day is filled already and you can't find the half hour necessary to ride every day, you will not be able to do as much for your body as someone who has the opportunity to ride more often. To keep your body in shape it must be exercised regularly. Regularly means at least every other day. If you already ride exclusively on weekends, you probably find that your ability and endurance are not what they should be. Your muscles, after five days of inactivity, cannot condition themselves to hard cycling in only two days time.

If you do not have the time to get out on the open road during the week, it would be more than worthwhile to invest in some training rollers. This also applies to people who are kept inside for long periods of time due to unfavorable weather. To keep those muscles fit and your body healthy there is nothing that can replace at least fifteen minutes of exercise every day. With training rollers you can exercise in the convenience of your own home.

EXERCISE PROGRAMS: Every person will have to develop his own cycling program. Even once it has been developed there will probably be need for change from time to time. It is not easy to judge the exact speed with which a person can best develop his body, and you will find out much about your capacities as your body starts to adjust to the exercise. At any rate, push yourself. Don't get lazy and quit before you have really given your body a workout. You should have a definite goal in mind and once you have attained that goal, you should keep up your distance and speed to keep your body in good health and capable of cycling with ease and efficiency over any distance that you care to traverse.

Just how far and how fast you develop in your program will depend to some extent on your age and physical condition. Be sure to design a program that will be within your capacity, and then stick to it. I will describe some average programs for different age groups to give you a basis for developing your own cycling program. These are by no means rigid and to be followed by everyone, but they can be used as a guide and will work well for most people.

Under 30

WEEK	BEGINNING		ENDING	
	miles	minutes	miles	minutes
1	3	12	3.5	14
2	4	16	4	15
3	4	15	4	14
4	4.5	16	4.5	15
5	5	18	5	17
6	5.5	20	5.5	19
7	6	22	6	21
8	6.5	24	6.5	23
9	7	26	7	25
10	7	24	7.5	28
11	7.5	27	7.5	26
12	8	29	8	28

30–40

WEEK	BEGINNING		ENDING	
	miles	minutes	miles	minutes
1	2	13	2	12
2	2.5	13	3	14
3	3	13	3.5	15
4	3.5	14	4	16
5	4	15	4.5	18
6	4.5	17	5	20
7	5	19	5	18
8	5.5	23	5.5	22
9	6	25	6	24
10	6.5	27	6.5	26
11	6.5	25	7	28
12	7	27	7.5	29
13	7.5	28	8	31
14	8	30		

GETTING IN SHAPE

40–50

WEEK	BEGINNING		ENDING	
	miles	minutes	miles	minutes
1	2	12	2	11
2	2.5	14	2.5	13
3	3	16	3	15
4	3.5	18	3.5	17
5	4	19	4	18
6	4.5	20	4.5	19
7	5	23	5	22
8	5	21	6	26
9	6	25	6	24
10	6.5	29	6.5	28
11	7	32	7	31
12	7	30	7.5	33
13	7.5	32	7.5	31
14	8	34	8	33
15	8	32		

OVER 50

WEEK	BEGINNING		ENDING	
	miles	minutes	miles	minutes
1	2	13	2	12
2	2.5	15	2.5	14
3	3	17	3	16
4	3.5	20	3.5	19
5	4	22	4	21
6	4.5	24	4.5	23
7	5	28	5	27
8	5	26	5.5	31
9	5.5	30	6	34
10	6	33	6	32
11	6.5	38	6.5	37
12	6.5	36	7	41
13	7	40	7.5	44
14	7.5	43	8	46
15	8	45	8.5	49
16	8.5	48	9	53
17	9	52	9.5	56
18	9.5	55	10	57
19	10	56		

RACING AND TOURING: If you are already in good physical condition and you plan to take up racing or touring, you will have to go beyond the exercise programs just outlined. These programs will be a good place to start, but you will have to work harder if you want to use your bicycle for more than just exercise. An experienced cyclist will cover the distances given in the exercise program just to get warmed up, and then go on to cycle another twenty miles.

All of the suggestions about preparation, warming up, and cooling down are even more important if you are going to ride farther and faster. Since you will have to make more stringent demands on your body, there will be even more need for proper preparation. The only real difference between training and exercise is one of degree. The basic principles are still the same.

Since racing demands much from the cyclist in terms of technique and stamina, the required training should have expert supervision. Anyone with an interest in bicycle racing should join a club or train under the supervision of a coach. Although it is possible to train on your own, there is no substitute for the many years of experience a good coach can pass on to an aspiring racer. Once you have raced for a few years you may develop methods and techniques of your own, but to start you should have someone with experience to guide you. There are very few competitors in any sport who can do without the guidance of a good coach.

There are as many theories on proper training as there are bicycle racers, but some generalizations can be made that will give anyone interested in racing some idea of what to expect. There are two aspects to bicycle racing: speed and endurance, which require two types of physical ability, strength and stamina. Most training programs are designed to increase both of these abilities.

To maintain and improve his stamina, a racing cyclist must ride a considerable distance every day. Most will ride for

GETTING IN SHAPE

upwards of three hours as a regular part of their training. The only way to build stamina is to ride. A good brisk pace over long distances is necessary to prepare a cyclist for the grueling demands of a bicycle race.

Aside from the long rides to increase stamina, a racing cyclist is constantly trying to improve his speed. Regular work with a stop watch is needed to cut seconds off the time it takes to cover certain distances. A competing cyclist should have an accurate estimation of his own speed under various circumstances in order to run an intelligent race and should always work to improve on his time.

Though most people will not have the strength, time, nor even the desire to race with their bicycles, touring is a facet of cycling that can be enjoyed by anyone with very little preparation. All avid cyclists engage in either racing or touring (they rarely do both). Since racing requires so much in the way of training and technique, the majority of bicycle owners take to the roads for the simple pleasure of just riding through miles and miles of beautiful scenery.

Although touring does not demand as much, physically, from the rider as racing, it does require a bit of training. Anyone who takes a trip with his bicycle should prepare himself for the miles that he will log. It would be foolish to start on a long ride without ever having gone farther than around the block. It is not difficult to travel long distances with a good bicycle, but you should work your way up to it gradually.

PROGRAMS FOR INCREASING CAPACITY: If you ride every day, it should take only a few weeks to prepare yourself for a long trip. Start by extending your daily ride and you will be in shape before you know it. Gradually work up to a brisk two-hour ride each day and it will be more than enough to get your riding muscles ready to take on mile after mile of open road. You should set a relaxed pace and try to maintain a steady cadence on each ride. Try to develop a smooth spin on your pedals regardless of whether you are going uphill or down. Hills should be included in your ride, but you should let your gears do the work in conquering them. This takes practice so don't be discouraged if you have to walk to the top during your first week or so. Once you can set and hold a good cycling rhythm, you will be able to span hill after hill without fatigue.

Once a week you should ride for at least 35 to 50 miles, and one week should include a 100-mile run. If you have never toured before, or if you like good company while riding, you should take advantage of the rides that are regularly scheduled by various cycling organizations: The League of American Wheelmen usually plans rides from 30 to 100 miles in length once a week; American Youth Hostels also organizes rides from 25 to 100 miles regularly. Since these rides are organized and led by experienced cyclists, they provide a good opportunity for the average bicycle rider to learn what touring is like. You can gain experience under good leadership while preparing to strike out on your own trip with your own itinerary. Much can be learned from others, and every cyclist should take advantage of the opportunity to learn more about his bicycle and his own cycling capabilities.

It is possible to increase your capacity by riding exclusively on weekends. You should start at least six weeks before your intended trip. If you ride healthy distances regularly you will not need any preparation other than what you will get once you are out on the road; but if you have never turned in a good day of sheer mileage, six weeks should be enough time to get in shape.

The first four weeks should be rides leading up to 100 miles. The first week you should ride 30 miles, the second 50, the third 75, and the fourth week 100. By taking a longer run each weekend than you did the week before, you will

GETTING IN SHAPE

gradually get your muscles in shape for the long rides on your trip. By the last two weekends, you should be taking 50-mile rides. By this time they should be fairly easy to cover without leaving you sore or fatigued when you are ready to start out on your tour.

Once you have prepared yourself for a trip and are ready to start out, you should take it easy for the first few days. Make sure you plan your trip so that you won't be rushed in the beginning. In spite of your preparation your body will still have to adjust to the constant riding and the daily mileage. If you take it easy and prepare yourself gradually, you will have an enjoyable trip instead of an exhausting experience.

Chapter 6

Rules of the Road

Bicyclists are subject to the same traffic laws which govern the drivers of automobiles. Every cyclist should know and follow the laws of the area in which he intends to ride; it could save him from a costly ticket or an even costlier accident. Traffic regulations are designed to ensure the safest possible flow of vehicles along public roads and adherence to them will make your journey a safe one. Every parent whose child has a bicycle should make sure that the child is familiar with the rules of the road and that he obeys them.

The first rule of safety when using any vehicle is to make sure that it is in good working condition. About 20 percent of all accidents involving bicycles are caused by faulty equipment. Always check your bicycle before you take it out on the street. Check the handlebars, pedals, wheels, gears, lights, and seat. Make sure that all parts are firmly in place and there are no loose bolts to fall out while you are actually riding. If something is loose, tighten it. If something must be replaced, do it before you take a chance on riding. Remember always that you are taking chances with your own safety, as well as the safety of others by riding on faulty equipment.

TRAFFIC LAWS: Always stop for red lights and stop signs. Even if there seem to be no cars in sight, you never know when someone is going to appear out of nowhere. It is also advisable to slow down at intersections where there are no traffic lights or stop signs. It is not enough to be right. You may conscientiously be following all traffic regulations—and someone else may not. Ride defensively. If some motorist is foolish enough to run a stop sign or a red light, make sure that you aren't in his way when he does.

You should be able to recognize all road signs by their shape. Stop signs are octagonal, yield signs are triangular, railroad-warning signs circular, speed signs are rectangular, and warning signs, diamond shaped.

As a general rule, it is better to yield the right of way to motorists regardless of whom it belongs to. If you clearly have the right of way and are positive that the other person is aware of it, you may avoid confusion by continuing, but never assume that you can proceed just because you are allowed to by law. Pedestrians always have the right of way and cyclists should grant it to them courteously.

Always signal your turns and stops. All signals should be made with the left arm extended straight from the shoulder when turning left, turned upward at the elbow for turning right, and turned down for stopping. These arm signals should be practiced by the novice until they can be made without losing control of his bicycle. Signal well in advance of the turn or stop, usually about 100 feet before reaching the intersection. If other drivers are aware of your intentions they can respond accordingly. This will eliminate much dangerous confusion.

Making a left turn in traffic can be a tricky accomplishment. Crossing traffic to get to the center of the road is dangerous and it is much better to avoid it. The safest way to turn left is to go straight through the intersection, thereby staying on the right side of the street. When you get to the other side, dismount and walk your bicycle across the street like a pedestrian. You are then ready to remount and continue on your way in the proper direction.

WHERE TO RIDE: Unless otherwise specified by law, cyclists should always keep to the right side of the road. This reduces the amount of impact if an accident should occur. It may be a bit disturbing to have cars passing you from behind but it won't take long for you to get used to the feeling and it is safer in the long run.

Stay off the sidewalks; they are the pedestrian's territory. In most states it is illegal to ride on sidewalks and you are likely to receive a ticket for doing so. If for any reason you are forced to use a sidewalk, do as the pedestrians do: dismount and walk your bike.

You should always ride on streets where there are parked cars in evidence. There are approximately three feet of space from a parked car to the nearest lane, and this is enough for a bicycle to pass safely. On streets where there are no parked cars, the right-hand lane will be used by motorists and there will not be enough room for them to allow a bicycle to pass; they will be forced to change lanes or follow along behind you at a pace to which they are unaccustomed.

If you are riding with a friend or a number of friends,

always ride in single file. Remember that there is enough room on most streets for one bicycle to pass safely; ride two abreast and there is none.

RIDING AT NIGHT: Nighttime riding can be a pleasure. There is usually less traffic at night than there is in the daytime and the reduced noise level is a blessing to any bicyclist. There are, however, differences encountered while cycling at night that you should know about and be prepared for.

The biggest disadvantage that arises when the sun goes down is the decreased visibility. You will not be able to see as well, and motorists will have difficulty seeing you unless you have the proper equipment. Lights are universally required for riding at night. You should have both a front and rear light and they should be visible to passing motorists for at least 300 feet. In addition to the two lights that are required by law, it is advisable to have as many reflectors as possible. Reflectors can easily be mounted on brake nuts, on the seat, on racks, on mudguards, and on the pedals. The pedals are a good place for reflectors since their constant movement draws attention to them and are more apt to be seen. They can also be strapped or clipped onto your trousers to give them movement. Reflectors mounted on arms or extended away from the bicycle are also a good idea. This positioning will give you an extra few inches of safety in case someone's judgment is bad.

Wear bright clothing at night. A lightweight nylon windbreaker of bright orange will not only help to keep you warm, it will help you be seen. An "X" across the back with reflective tape will also help. In fact, you can put reflective tape almost anywhere on your bicycle or your clothing and it will add a little extra protection.

You also have to be careful about where you choose to ride at night. The cover of darkness has been used by the shadier elements of every society since the beginning of time. Parks, dimly lit streets, and secluded areas are not especially safe for anyone at night, including bicyclists. If nothing else, you may end up with your bicycle being stolen. Bicycle thieves are thriving these days, and no cyclist is immune. It is much better to avoid dangerous situations even if it means taking a little extra time to reach your destination. It could save your life.

RAIN AND FOG: Riding in the rain is not particularly hazardous if you take the rain into consideration. Wet pavement is slippery, especially during the first half hour of rain. If caught in the rain, slow down considerably on turns. Your rear wheel will have a tendency to slip out from under you if you try to corner your bicycle in the same way that you do when the roads are dry. You should approach any stops with caution. Slow down gradually and then brake easily. If your brakes grab too fast, which they will have a tendency to do when wet, your back wheel will skid and you may lose control of the bicycle. If you do start to skid, let up on the brake momentarily and, when you feel in control once again, apply pressure on the brake in short pulses. This will keep the rear wheel from sliding.

Fog, especially at night, can make it difficult to see anything. It is better not to ride in fog, but if you cannot avoid it turn your front light down a bit so that it shines on the road a few yards in front of your bicycle. Fog reflects light and this will keep your light from being projected back at you and impairing your ability to see. Remember that automobile drivers will have an even harder time seeing you than on the darkest of nights.

HAZARDS: There are certain hazards that you should look out for even under the most ideal riding conditions. A cyclist, like everyone else who uses public roads, must stay alert and ready to avoid any obstacle that might jeopardize his safety. Taking spills can be a painful experience and can cause considerable damage to your bicycle.

Watch out for storm drains. The grating allows just enough room for a front bicycle wheel to drop through, sending the rider over the handlebars to continue on his own. These drains are not always easy to spot, especially at night, and they can cause a great deal of damage to your front wheel.

Although streets with parked cars are the safest to ride on, they do present a particular problem for the bicyclist. Drivers often leave their cars by opening the door towards the street. If they do, it will place a rather sudden barrier directly in your path. It is therefore advisable to be on the alert and spot this situation in advance. You should also be wary of drivers who pull out of parking spaces without bothering to signal. Always watch to see if any of the cars on the street are occupied. If they are, approach with caution.

Be careful when approaching driveways. You never know when someone is going to pull out right in front of you. Also be careful of pedestrians who may cross the street from behind any number of obstacles. If you can't see because of an obstacle, slow down.

Keep an eye out for cars making right turns at intersections. Since they must turn from the right-hand lane, they will cross directly in your path. If they do not notice you and you're not on the alert, there is liable to be a collision.

Since you will be riding on the side of the road, watch out for the debris which tends to collect there. Broken bottles, cans, pieces of automobile tires, and numerous other articles are discarded on the streets every day. If you spot them in time you may save yourself a sizable repair bill.

DOS AND DON'TS: Never ride two on a bike unless you have one that is built for that express purpose. Bicycles that are made for one rider cannot safely carry two. The added weight and increased instability will make it difficult to control your bicycle under normal conditions, and could cause serious problems if an emergency should arise.

Never try to hitch a ride by hanging onto a truck, bus, or any other motorized vehicle. It is extremely dangerous. You cannot predict what the driver is going to do and if he should turn or stop suddenly, you are in for a grueling experience. Ride under your own power; after all, that is what you are riding a bicycle for. If you want to be motorized, buy a vehicle that has its own motor.

Always ride in a straight line. Don't weave back and forth. Clowning around should be reserved for those times when you have your feet on the ground. The minute you put your feet on the pedals, you are involved in a serious endeavor and should take it seriously. Riding in a straight line will reduce the possibility of getting hit by a passing motorist and will make it easier for you to respond to any emergency that may arise.

Never try to adjust or repair anything on your bicycle while riding. You should always check your bike before you set out, but if something should go wrong, pull over to a safe place and make the needed adjustments. You cannot watch the road and fix your bicycle at the same time, so don't attempt it.

ETIQUETTE: One should always try to be courteous and considerate while riding. If more people followed this basic principle, there would be less tension and fewer accidents on public streets. It is hard to keep up the good smile when motorists are honking and screaming as if they own the roads, but, in a way they do! It would help tremendously if roads would ever be adapted to accommodate bicycles as well as automobiles. In the meantime, everyone is going to have to do his best to make a bad situation tolerable. There has to be a feeling of cooperation on the part of everyone who shares the space allotted to the public for transportation. A little friendliness in the face of adversity may help to keep the cooperation at a maximum.

If you should come across another cyclist who is having difficulties, stop, and ask if you can be of any service. Maybe he only needs a certain tool that he forgot to carry with him, or a spare part that he doesn't have. Maybe he could use some helpful knowledge. Maybe, someday, you will be in the same situation. You can learn a lot from other cyclists and there is no better way to get to know them than by lending a hand in a time of need.

Chapter 7

Picking Local Routes

Since streets are not designed for the exclusive use of the cyclist, some degree of planning is necessary to find those streets which afford the greatest amount of safety. Side streets are generally better suited to the cyclist's needs than main thoroughfares. Freeways and tollways should always be avoided. It is against the law to ride on them with a bicycle, anyway. Main highways should be forsaken for the less crowded and more scenic roads. Streets that run parallel to main thoroughfares should be investigated for use by cyclists.

Any street with heavy traffic should be avoided as much as possible. The noise and confusion alone are enough to make most cyclists seek other routes. When you add to this unpleasantness the danger that is always present on a crowded street, picking side streets to travel is well worth the time and effort.

MAPS: Although maps cannot replace the experience of first-hand knowledge of the best streets to travel, they do provide a good place to start for anyone who plans to cycle in his own town or city. Maps make it possible to take in large areas at a glance, and a little knowledge of how to read maps can help you find streets suitable for your use.

It is a good idea to use more than one map. A map of the general area in which you live is good to have if you want to travel any distance and aren't familiar with the surrounding territory. Detailed and smaller maps with a larger scale will be of more help in picking the actual streets you will use. You can get a better idea of just what kind of streets are available from a map that covers less territory and gives greater detail.

Maps of your area can be obtained from the city or county offices which publish maps for sale to the general public. To find out what office is responsible for map publication in your area, you should call the city or county public relations department. They will be able to direct you to the correct office. Your local chamber of commerce may also publish maps which are designed to give information on points of local interest. Parks, historical sites, museums, zoos, and recreational facilities are available in any area, and a knowledge of their whereabouts and importance will make your cycling time as enjoyable as possible. Become a tourist in your own community and see what you can discover.

If you belong to the Automobile Club of America, or if you have a friend who does, you will find it an excellent source for maps and information. The Automobile Club supplies assistance for thousands of travelers every year, and they will be able to help you get the most from your travels within your own community. They also furnish information on points of interest, dining facilities, and emergency information. A visit to the local office of the community in which you live will help you pick those routes from which you will derive the most benefit.

All maps have a legend designed to inform the map reader what the different symbols used on the map stand for. There is usually a scale that tells you what distance on the map represents what distance on the ground. Streets and highways are marked by different kinds of lines for different types of roads enabling you to see quickly the kind of street you are looking at. The mileage between various points is sometimes given in red along the road which connects the points. Recreation areas may also be marked, but there are usually no details given about these areas unless you have a map designed for that specific purpose.

PICKING ROUTES: As has been suggested, you should avoid busy streets if possible. Side streets are quieter and safer. They will give you less to worry about and more to enjoy. In most cities, there are side streets that run parallel to main thoroughfares, and you should get to know what these streets are. People usually form a general idea of how they can get around the area they live in by familiarizing themselves with the larger streets. The same process can be used to discover side streets. Maps will be useful in planning which streets you will travel, but a good first-hand knowledge of how to get around should become a part of bicycling in your own city.

If you are not sure whether or not a street is suitable for riding, such as whether or not parking is allowed, you can call your local traffic division and ask them for the information you need. Some streets are also rated as to the traffic flow, and the department may be able to give you some idea of how much traffic to expect, but the best way to find out which streets are best for cycling is to cover the city yourself.

Local bicycle organizations can give you information as to

the best places in your community for bicycling. The League of American Wheelmen, the American Youth Hostels, and local cycling clubs have already put in many hours of practical research by planning and executing rides for their own organizations which they will gladly pass on. Another good source of information may be your local bicycle shop. If the personnel do any cycling themselves, and they probably do, they will be able to give you some helpful hints as to the best streets to travel.

Chapter 8

Preparing for a Trip

Once you have decided to buy a bicycle, you will probably want to travel with it, sooner or later. To get the most from your purchase, you should at least spend a day with it once in a while. Even short excursions into areas that lie outside your own town or city will provide a richly rewarding experience.

A pleasant and trouble-free trip must be well planned. The bicycle should be in top running condition and thoroughly checked before you start out. You should know what route you plan to take as well as have a general idea of alternate routes in case you are forced to take a detour. You should carry tools, spare parts, emergency kits, and extra clothing with you, but you have to be careful not to burden your bicycle with excess weight.

If you plan to do any extensive traveling by bicycle, you should seriously consider investing in one with a ten-speed derailleur gear changer. It is not altogether impossible to cover long distances with a three-speed bicycle, but you will more than likely be so fatigued by the time you have reached your destination that you will be in no shape to enjoy yourself. With ten different gear ratios to choose from, you can travel easily and maintain a respectable cycling speed for days on end and without regard to terrain.

PREPARING YOURSELF: It would be foolish to plan a trip, secure and pack all your necessary items, and prepare your bicycle, if you are not in shape to cycle the distance. Your body needs preparation well in advance. Before you actually start out on a tour you should train your muscles and develop your bicycling technique so that you will be able to ride long distances without putting undue strain on your body. You should start training a few weeks before you intend to leave. If you are planning an extended tour, more preparation time may be necessary. Start by extending your daily ride and, gradually, work towards covering greater distances at better speeds than you are normally used to.

It would also be a good idea to load your saddlebags and panniers with some weight so you can accustom yourself to having a heavier bicycle. You will discover that it is not as easy to corner a loaded bicycle at high speeds without risking a spill. You will also have to change your gearing technique. You will find that the added weight forces you to change gears sooner than you were used to when approaching a hill. The added weight will also increase your momentum when going downhill, thus decreasing your braking ability.

PREPARING THE BICYCLE: Before you are ready to take a trip, your bicycle must be taken apart, cleaned, reassembled, and properly adjusted. Your wheel bearings, crank bearings, head bearings, pedal bearings, and derailleur bearings must be cleaned and regreased. Your wheels should be properly aligned and there should be no drag or wobble due to maladjustment. Derailleurs should be aligned and adjusted and your chain should be removed and cleaned. Any misalignment, dirt, or improper lubrication will produce unwanted drag and could cause your bicycle to be damaged while out on the road.

Any worn or broken parts should be replaced. If you have to replace parts when you're on the road, it will be much more difficult to do than if you had replaced them before you left. Check your brakes and brake cables thoroughly. If your brake cables are worn or bent they should be replaced. Brake pads that are worn out or old should be traded in for new ones.

Tires should be checked thoroughly. If something looks amiss, you won't actually have to replace the tire, but you should be prepared to do so while on the road. Clincher tires are more durable and easier to repair than tubular tires. If you plan to take your bicycle through uncharted territory or along rocky footpaths, they are probably a better tire to have. If you plan to stick to the roads, you are better off using tubulars. Because they are lighter, tubulars are easier to ride on than clinchers. You can also carry an extra tubular, tire and all, strapped underneath your seat, making repairs on the road unnecessary. All you have to do is replace the flat tire with a new one and then you can repair the flat at your leisure when you stop for the night.

Make sure that the seat and handlebars are adjusted for the best possible ease in riding. You should be able to sit comfortably with your weight properly distributed between the seat, handlebars, and the pedals. Never start a tour with a new saddle. You should have a saddle that is well broken in if you don't want to develop blisters in inconvenient places. The best saddle is made of leather because leather conforms to the shape of the body after use and is the most comfortable seat once it has been broken in. It should be narrow to prevent your thighs from chafing as you pedal. Any rubbing against your thighs will be a painful experience when you still have many miles left to pedal.

Your seat should be adjusted so that your heel just rests on the pedal when your legs are extended on either side of the bicycle. If the seat is too high or too low, it will greatly decrease your cycling efficiency. Many scientific studies have been conducted which prove a direct relationship between the saddle height and the efficiency of the pedaling. With proper saddle height you will be able to pedal properly. If you even want to get more accurate about this adjustment, the height of the saddle should be 1.09 times the length of your leg measured from the crotch to the floor. If you are used to an improper saddle height, it may take awhile to get used to the new position, but it will be well worthwhile to get into good habits.

ACCESSORIES: To carry all of your tools, kits, maps, clothing, food, and spare parts, you will need at least one bag, and possibly more, depending on the length of the trip and the style in which you intend to travel. If you are only going to be gone for a day, you can probably get by with just a saddlebag and a few pockets, provided you make good use of your space and don't carry unnecessary items. If you plan to take your own food or if one bag isn't enough, a handlebar bag should add more than enough space for the needed items.

If you plan any extensive touring or camping, you will need front and rear panniers as well as bags. Even for short trips it is a good idea to have panniers as well as a saddlebag because this enables you to distribute the weight of your gear evenly along the length of the bicycle. An evenly distributed load makes the bicycle easier to ride.

With your bags and panniers you should have bag supports.

Supports keep the equipment from becoming entangled in the wheels and causing damage to the bicycle. Supports will also help keep your bags in good condition by reducing the amount of stress they must carry.

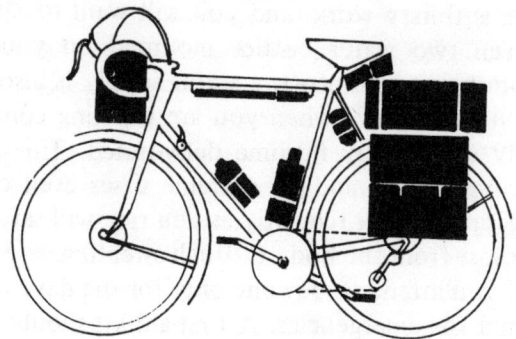

Bicycle Loaded with Camping Gear
Figure 7.

Rattrap pedals and cleats on your shoes are almost necessary for touring. They enable you to keep your feet firmly planted on the pedals when pushing over hills. Without having your feet anchored securely, you run the risk of having your foot slip off and causing an annoying spill. Spills can quickly spoil a pleasurable ride by damaging the bicycle, the gear, the rider, or all three.

If you are going to have cleated shoes for cycling, and it is strongly advised, you should also take a pair of slip-on shoes to be used for walking. Cleats should not be used for walking, and a pair of loafers or sneakers will enable you to change quickly from your cycling feet to your walking feet. Another pair of shoes will also be a pleasant change for your feet after you have cycled any appreciable distance.

If you happen to have any difficulties on the road you may not be able to return before dark, so you should always be prepared for nighttime riding, even if you only plan to be gone for the day. You should have a front and a rear light and they should be in good working condition. Your lights should always be checked before you leave on a trip. Spare batteries and bulbs should be packed among your replacement parts and you should even carry a small flashlight in case of failure.

Cycling is thirsty work, and you will want to carry one or maybe even two water bottles mounted on your bicycle. Aside from being a comfort, a water supply is also an aid to health. On a hot day, when you are pedaling continuously, your body can rapidly become dehydrated. This can affect your cycling ability and in extreme cases even cause heat cramps. Sipping water regularly as you ride will safely replace the water lost from the body through sweating.

Even if you intend to be gone only for the day, you should be prepared for emergencies. A first-aid kit should be carried on your bicycle at all times. A basic first-aid kit (such as the one described in the chapter on first aid) should be a regular part of your gear if you wish to be prepared for an accident.

A tool kit is a must. You cannot make repairs without tools and repairs often have to be made on the road. You should have a list of all the tools necessary for your bicycle and you should make sure that you include these tools when you are packing your gear.

Nailpullers are also handy to have if you are going to do any touring with your bicycle. They will help minimize the number of flat tires that you will have to stop to repair.

CLOTHING: Any good clothing for cycling will be fine on a long ride. If it is warm weather you should probably wear lightweight cycling shorts. Long pants are not as suited to ease in cycling as shorts. The restriction that long pants put on your leg movements will be of no help for easy cycling. An extra pair of long pants that can be slipped over the shorts should be taken along in case you want to do any hiking while on the road or in case the weather turns cold.

A lightweight riding jersey or pullover shirt should be

worn. Shirts with buttons should be avoided if possible. Buttons have a habit of falling off at the most inopportune time. In addition, the shirt should preferably be made of material that gives with body movement yet stays close to the skin. This will give you freedom of movement and minimize the amount of perspiration while riding. You should also carry a sweater in case the weather should turn cold or you get stranded somewhere after the sun goes down.

A lightweight windbreaker should be available for cool days or riding done during the evening hours. A heavy coat shouldn't be necessary. With a sweater and a windbreaker you should stay perfectly warm while cycling.

Riding gloves should be worn to prevent blisters and protect your hands. You should also have a pair of mittens for cold-weather cycling.

A riding cap with a sun visor will help reduce glare and prevent sunburned noses. Sunglasses should also be worn. It is hard to see anything else when the sun bounces off mile after mile of pavement and into your eyes, so you should try to minimize this effect.

FOOD: When planning a trip, you should include plans for food. Whether you are going to eat in restaurants or carry your own food with you, be sure that you will not have trouble once you are on the road. If you are traveling on a Sunday or a holiday, remember that it may not be possible to find stores or restaurants that are open. This is not much of a problem in big cities, but since most cyclists don't plan their rides through big cities, it should be taken into consideration.

The best way to obtain food while you are traveling by bicycle is to carry it with you. That way you will not have to worry about whether or not you are going to find supplies and you will not have to stay close to populated areas. You will be able to stop to eat whenever you feel hungry and in whatever surroundings strike your fancy. You may get a bit hungry so be sure to carry enough food to sustain your energy. An average person needs 3,500 calories during a day of cycling and your food should be planned to supply this caloric count. Any food you select should also be easy to digest and easy to prepare, if not already prepared.

If you are going to be gone for one day, all you will have to carry with you is your lunch and a couple of snacks. You should eat a good hot breakfast before leaving in the morning and you can eat supper when you return at night. It is better, when cycling, to eat often and in small amounts rather than to stuff yourself for lunch in hopes that it will carry you through the rest of the day. You should stop to eat as soon as you feel the first signs of hunger. Don't wait until you are half starved before stocking up on energy. Some fresh fruit midway between breakfast and lunch will give you energy and keep your appetite from getting the better of you when lunch finally rolls around. For lunch you should have something light like a sandwich and possibly a cup of soup. After lunch you should have another snack if you get hungry before you reach your destination. Do not carry unnecessary food, but make sure that you will not be famished when you still have miles left to pedal.

If you are going to cycle in uncharted areas or are going to be out on the road for any length of time, you should carry an emergency supply of rations. Army surplus "K" and "C" rations or other dehydrated foods can be stored indefinitely and are easy and light to carry. Dehydrated foods are also a good way to eat in nonemergency situations. A cyclist can carry complete and varied meals that will last for weeks without taking up too much space in his panniers.

PLANNING THE ROUTE: When planning the route you will take, you should be careful to avoid traveling on major highways. Pick roads that parallel these highways and cross them in as few places as possible. Not only are highways

PREPARING FOR A TRIP

designed for straight-through traffic and thus are not very scenic, they are rather dangerous as well. Stick to the roads that wind through small towns and pleasant countryside. It will make the trip pleasanter and more worthwhile.

Before embarking on any trip you should estimate as nearly as possible how much distance you can cover in a certain amount of time. In order to do this you will have to have a rough idea of what the terrain is like that you are going to be traveling over. Use a topographical map to judge approximately whether or not you will be going uphill or down. It is a good idea to divide your route into sections of uphill, downhill, and level stretches before you leave. In this manner you can estimate correctly just where you will be at any given time. Your itinerary shouldn't be a binding time schedule, but you should be able to estimate quickly how long it will take you to cover a certain distance on the map once you are on the road. Remember that uphill grades will take longer than downhill grades.

It is also a good idea to have alternate routes in mind in case you are forced from your original plans. Maps are not always up-to-date and roads are closed for many reasons at any time of the year. Detours are usually marked on closed roads, but they are marked for automobile traffic and not for the cyclist. Before taking a detour you should have a good idea of what type of roads it will take you over.

CAMPING EQUIPMENT: If you plan any extensive touring or even a weekend ride now and then, you can increase your pleasure considerably by combining it with a bit of camping. By equipping yourself to the point of being a self-contained unit, you can stop and stay wherever you feel like staying without having to stay close to populated areas.

Your tent should be a sewn-in floor type. This will give you the best possible protection from the annoying effects of weather and insects. It should have a door flap with a zip-up mosquito netting. It is hard to keep your tent flap closed on warm nights, and even harder to keep the insects out if you have no netting on your tent.

Your sleeping bag should be made of down to keep weight at a minimum and warmth at a maximum. It should not be waterproof. Your tent floor will more than take care of any outside moisture, and a waterproof sleeping bag would keep body moisture from escaping, leaving you damp. Moisture is deadly on a cold night. You will stay warm and dry in a down bag.

If you do not like to be kept awake nights by sleeping on hard ground, an air mattress can also be included. However, air mattresses are usually unreliable as well as bulky, and it is quite a job to expel all the air from it when packing. It would be better to carry a foam pad that you can roll up and compress easily. The pad will not afford as much protection from the hard ground as an air mattress, but it will do adequately and does not weigh very much.

Other camping items will have to be included if you intend to do any cooking. A good mess kit and a canteen will be needed, and if you are not going to build campfires, you will need a camp stove. I would forgo the stove, which is bulky and not very reliable, for a waterproof matchbox and a good supply of matches.

CHECKLISTS: Checklists for planning a trip are included in the appendix, but they are only rough guides. Everyone soon discovers which items he will use and which are not needed for his own personal comfort. Once you have taken a few trips, you may want to add or subtract items that you found either useful or useless. Not everyone travels with the same ideas of comfort and necessity, so you should develop your own list as you go along. Make sure that you write out a list of needed items when planning a trip. It is much easier to check items off on a piece of paper than to try to remember whether or not everything is packed.

PACKING: When packing your gear, remember to distribute the weight as evenly as possible. Uneven weight distribution will make your bicycle difficult to ride.

Try as much as possible to keep all your items light in weight. Don't take aerosol cans, but use plastic bottles instead. Take a small bar of soap. You can usually buy more soap while on the road. This holds true for all other toilet articles. Put individual items in plastic bags and label them for easy access when on the road.

Remember to pack those items that you will use frequently in easy reach. Don't put your maps in the bottom of your bag because you will have a hard time finding them when you need them. Wise packing will save you much time and trouble once you have started your trip.

Chapter 9

Hosteling

Hosteling is an inexpensive and enlightening way to travel. Hostels are maintained throughout the world where members can obtain overnight lodging and cooking privileges for a reasonable fee. Aside from providing and maintaining hostels in the United States, the American Youth Hostel Association (a non-profit organization) also provides many services for the cyclist who never intends to travel or use a hostel.

The name American Youth Hostels is slightly misleading. It is by no means an organization designed for the exclusive use of youthful cyclists. People of all ages are members and participate in the activities sponsored by AYH. There are currently 52,000 AYH passholders in the United States and the worldwide hosteling membership totals 1,940,000.

Hosteling is open to anyone who enjoys the outdoors and travel of any kind. Whether you travel by backpack, bicycle, canoe, or even motorized vehicles, you can obtain lodging in a relaxed friendly atmosphere with other members whose interests are the same as yours.

HISTORY: Hosteling was originated in 1909 by a German schoolteacher named Richard Schirrmann to give his students an opportunity to leave the city occasionally and discover some of the beauties of nature. He took them on hikes through the countryside, but was always faced with the problem of obtaining suitable overnight shelter. He developed the idea of establishing clean, inexpensive hostels for traveling students where they could rest for the night in comfort and safety.

Richard Schirrmann's school became the first hostel and, in only two years, the idea had spread through Germany. With the help and contributions of many interested citizens, seventeen hostels were established that could be used by young people when hiking through the country. As the idea of hosteling spread to other countries the need arose for a governing body that would establish a consistent set of rules and regulations. In 1932, an international hosteling conference met in Holland. A plan was formulated which provided uniformity of procedure and enabled hostelers to travel from one country to another. Each country agreed to recognize a pass issued in any other member country and standards of health, sanitation, and safety were established. The rules still stand today in hostels throughout the world.

The first hostel was established in the United States in 1934 and the AYH has been growing ever since. It has provided services for travelers in an ever-expanding effort to promote travel and all forms of outdoor activity related to travel. The organization is now working on a chain of hostels that would extend across the United States along three different routes and would space hostels only 300 miles apart. This will make it possible for AYH members to travel practically anywhere in the United States with ease.

HOSTELS: The name hostel comes from an old word meaning inn. A hostel is an overnight accommodation, usually located in scenic or historical areas, where resident houseparents provide lodging and supervision for a variety of different travelers. The hostel may be a church, school, farmhouse, or a building put up specifically to accommodate lodgers. In Europe the hostel may be a castle, a mountain lodge, a villa, or even a converted sailing ship.

Basically, hostels consist of a sleeping area, a dining area or kitchen facilities, and a hostel common room. The common room is a good place to meet and get to know travelers from all over the world. It is designed to allow a free exchange of ideas between people of all races and nationalities. Many enjoyable hours can be spent learning from the experiences of other people in the convivial atmosphere of a hostel.

There are currently forty-seven countries represented in the International Youth Hostel Federation and they maintain a total of 4,200 hostels throughout the world. In the United States and Canada there are 139 hostels for the use of members and more are being established every year. Members are supplied with a list of the hostels, and a pass from one country is honored in the hostels of all other member countries.

HOW TO JOIN: To join AYH you should write to the AYH council nearest you (see appendix for addresses). If you live in a city that maintains an office, you can pick up an application form in person. The membership fee for one year is $5 for anyone under eighteen, $10 for an individual over eighteen, and $12 for a family which includes children under eighteen; but these fees are only good in the United States and Canada. A special individual youth pass can be obtained for $2 by applicants under eighteen, in groups of ten or more, if an official of their church, school, boy scout or boys' club organization files the application. The special individual youth pass is only valid in the United States. Life membership for an individual costs $50.

HOW TO HOSTEL: If you plan to use the hostels provided by AYH on a bicycle tour, you will need an AYH *Hostel Guide and Handbook.* This can be ordered through AYH for $1.25 but is sent free to members. It will list the locations of all the youth hostels in the United States and also supply such information as how to hostel, what equipment you will need, how to take care of a bicycle, and how to obtain maps. With the guide, you will be able to plan at which hostels you are going to stay and write ahead for reservations.

A pass is issued with membership that is good in any hostel. You must present this pass to the houseparent before you register. The pass should contain a photograph of yourself which you will have to paste in yourself. A sleeping bag is also required. The sleeping bag can be purchased through AYH and must be shown with your pass.

Many hostelers buy their own food and do their own cooking. They also do their own cleaning up so be prepared to pitch in and help. You should have your own eating utensils and dish towel since these are not supplied at the hostel.

Making reservations in advance insures the traveler that he will have a bed upon arriving at the hostel. With reservations you should arrive at the hostel between 5 and 7 p.m. A person traveling alone can usually get a bunk without a reservation if he arrives before 5 p.m. You should leave the hostel by 9:30 a.m. Hostels are closed between 9:30 a.m. and 4:30 p.m. unless there is an emergency. The washing and cooking facilities are opened between 12:00 and 1:30 p.m.

for families staying more than one night. Anyone else using these facilities is charged $.25.

Your overnight hostel fee should be paid before you sign the register. It ranges from $1.50 to $2.00, with the exception of ski hostels during the ski season, in which case the fee may run as high as $3.00. Hostels abroad range from $.40 to $1.25.

WHAT TO EXPECT: Hostels are run on a traveler's schedule. They are designed to provide a good night's sleep and a fresh early start the next morning. Lights are out early and the rising time is usually 7:00 a.m. In fact, a good friend of mine tells of an experience in a hostel he stayed at while traveling through Europe. He had arrived late in the night with his traveling companions because of some difficulties on their way, and they did not get to sleep until well past midnight. They were rather amazed to be awakened at 5:00 a.m. by a German cycling club conducting their morning calisthenics in the dormitory room. Needless to say, this is not necessarily a common experience, but early to bed and early to rise is the prevailing custom in hostels.

As in any situation that makes it necessary for people of different types and backgrounds to get together for the first time, common courtesy prevails. The atmosphere is polite, hospitable, and highly conducive to the exchange and interplay of ideas. In common rooms throughout the world travel stories are passed from member to member. There are many different types of people to meet, but they all have one thing in common, a spirit of adventure that leads them into the out-of-doors whenever they get the opportunity. Much can be learned by seeing different lands through the eyes of someone else who has traveled through or lived in them.

Drinking is not allowed in hostels. Since they are designed to afford people the opportunity to grow healthy and knowledgeable through close communion with nature, alcoholic beverages are not considered in good taste. Smoking is restricted to the common room for reasons of hygiene and safety.

TRAVEL GROUPS: Aside from supplying overnight accommodations, the AYH sponsors over fifty hosteling trips each summer through its travel department. Trips by bicycle, often Volkswagen, chartered bus, and public transportation are led by trained and experienced hostelers. If you like to travel in a group or want expert guidance for your first trip, these AYH sponsored travel groups will be ideal. Generally speaking, the local councils of AYH plan shorter trips (lasting from two days to four weeks) while the longer trips are planned by the AYH National Headquarters to last from three to seven weeks in the United States, Mexico, and Canada. Trips to Europe, Israel, and Japan range from four to eight weeks. Prices for guided trips cost from $240 to $1100.

If you want to form your own travel group, AYH will provide expenses for the leader and either plan the itinerary or provide help in planning it. AYH is a good source of information for any person who enjoys and participates in travel.

OTHER ACTIVITIES: Even if you never intend to travel with your bicycle or use any of the hostels provided for such travel, AYH may still be able to provide you with many benefits. AYH is an organization that promotes healthy recreation on all levels and they are especially concerned with cycling, it being one of the best ways for most people to get out among the charms of nature.

One of the benefits of AYH membership is its qualification rides for cyclists. These are rides through scenic areas which give the cyclist a chance to test his cycling abilities at varying levels of difficulty. The rides are designed to cover a certain distance in a certain amount of time. The easiest ride is 25

HOSTELING

miles in 3 hours, and the rides progress in difficulty to 50 miles in 5 hours, 75 miles in 7 hours, and 100 miles in 10 and 8 hours. The routes include a variety of terrain and you can choose from different routes throughout the year. It is a great opportunity to test your own cycling ability as well as enjoy the companionship of other cyclists on an enjoyable ride. Friendly competition on the longer runs is also encouraged. AYH issues shoulder patches for the successful completion of a qualification ride. A cyclist can start with a less strenuous ride and work his way up to a 100-mile shoulder patch.

The local councils of AYH also establish seminars from time to time on various aspects of outdoor travel. Classes on bicycles, including repairs and maintenance, backpacking, and camping are offered to members of AYH. These classes can benefit the weekend cyclist who takes an interest in how he can get the most from the bicycle he owns.

The AYH council publications supply their readers with a wealth of information on cycling activities. Classes and club events are publicized regularly. There is information on bicycle racing, and regularly scheduled rides are described in detail. Lectures, including movies and slides that can be of help to any cyclist, are regularly scheduled. All in all, a good knowledge of what is happening in or near your community in terms of group activity can be obtained which will give you the opportunity to get the most from your bicycle.

The councils located in major cities also promote the development of AYH clubs in local areas. If there is no council near you, there may be an AYH club which sponsors its own activities in conjunction with and in the interest of promoting the same ideals as the AYH councils. If you are interested in its benefits, you should check with the council nearest you to see if there is a club in your community. If there is no AYH club you may want to start one. All you need are prospective members and some prospective activities. AYH will help to explain the activities of their organization by supplying a speaker for the first meeting of interested people. They will also help to draw up a constitution for the club and, if needed, even supply a qualified leader for the first trip. AYH also has training programs for those who want to lead groups on adventurous and enjoyable outings. Scholarships are available that will pay for the cost of the training.

AYH also books passage on ships to all parts of the world for those who are interested in overseas travel. Books and guides to European travel are available that include menu translators, charts for currency exchange, tips on tipping, charts for figuring European clothing sizes, and emergency information for traveling in foreign countries. These kits are reasonably priced and are an invaluable aid to anyone planning a trip abroad with their bicycle.

Other publications are also available through AYH that would be of benefit to a cyclist. A complete catalogue of publications can be obtained from AYH. Books on different aspects of travel and touring are available to the general public.

Chapter 10

Know the Way

Most people have had occasion to use a map at some time or another in their lives, yet most people know very little about them. There are a variety of maps available that supply a variety of information. Though you may be quite familiar with an area and perfectly capable of finding your way around, there is still certain information that you can gain by knowing how to read and use a map correctly. Maps are not reserved for the exclusive use of those who are lost or have to wind their way through unfamiliar territory. Though maps are certainly necessary for planning which roads you will travel, they can also give the cyclist knowledge that will be of benefit in planning time schedules and selecting the best possible routes in terms of scenery, ease of cycling, and recreational facilities.

TYPES OF MAPS: There are many different types of maps in existence, but the two that will be used almost exclusively by the cyclist are road maps and topographical maps. Every cyclist should know the function of both types and should be able to use the two together when planning cycle trips.

Road maps are relatively easy to read and even easier to find. They are distributed by most of the major oil companies and can be obtained at almost any gas station. As the name implies, a road map is a representation of the roads that crisscross the area covered by the map. For a more detailed description of a specific area you may want to use a county map. These, generally, have a larger scale and greater detail than the state maps that you find at gas stations. County maps can be obtained through the county or state agencies that publish maps for sale to the public. Just which agency is responsible for this service will depend upon what area of the country you are traveling through. The Department of the Interior publishes county maps whose scale is 1/4" to the mile. You may want to use a state map or even a map of the United States to plan your overall route, but for locating specific roads to travel a county map will be better suited to your purposes.

Topographic maps are not as common as road maps because they are of little use to motorists. To the cyclist they are useful. A topographic map is a representation of the topography of the earth. These maps make it possible for the cyclist to estimate the gradients along the route he intends to travel. With a topographic map you can get a general idea of how many hills you will have to climb and just how steep they are. You can also get a fair idea of what type of land you will be cycling through, whether it is mountain, flatland, or rolling hills.

Since you can judge the gradient along your route with a topographical map, you will also be able to estimate cycling time between distances more accurately than with only a road map. With the knowledge that you travel slower when going uphill and faster when going downhill, you can use a topographic map to see at which point along your prospective route you will lose or gain in your traveling time. If you are making reservations and have a schedule to keep, this kind of planning is indispensable.

Topographic maps are published by the Geological Survey and can be obtained through the Forest or National Park Service or by writing to the Superintendent of Documents, Washington, D.C. and requesting a topographical map index. This index can then be used in ordering the maps that you will be using.

HOW TO READ A MAP: Reading road maps is no insurmountable problem. All you have to do is look at the key provided with the map and learn which symbols represent what objects on the ground. Roads are clearly marked with different types of lines representing different types of roads. Even if you have never used a road map before in your life, you will be able to familiarize yourself quickly with the basic knowledge required to read one. It is not really convenient to keep glancing at the key every time you look at the map so it would be advisable to sit down and study the key for a few minutes. You will have no trouble memorizing the different symbols and it will save you time and trouble when you have to read your maps when you are on the road.

Topographical maps may take a little practice to read if you have never used one before. These are maps containing contour lines that connect points on the map that are at approximately the same altitude with respect to some standard altitude (usually sea level); they are drawn at regular intervals of elevation (or, one every twenty-five feet). Natural expressions of contours can be seen on shorelines, cultivated terraces, and the patterns produced by contour plowing. Index contours (generally every fifth line) are marked with their elevation written in and drawn in more heavily than the contour lines in between. Although the most frequent interval between contour lines is about 25 feet, intervals of 5, 10, 40, 50, 100, and 200 feet are also used if it is necessary to represent the topography of the land being mapped with greater clarity. Since contour lines represent the same elevation at all points along the line, they never intersect.

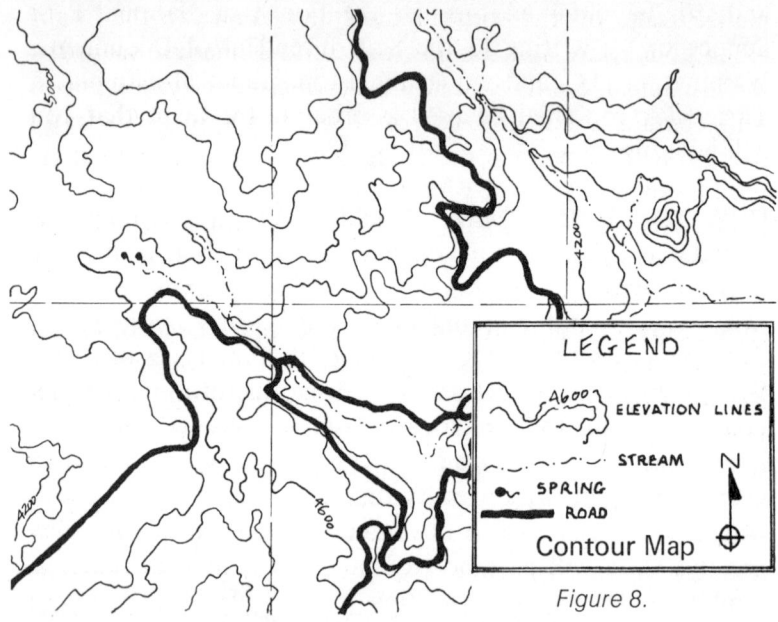

Figure 8.

All you will need to know to obtain a general idea of the gradients in any area is that contour lines, if closely spaced, represent steep slopes and contours that are far apart represent gentle slopes. To determine whether the slope is uphill or down, you will have to check the elevations of the lines on the map to see if the numbers are rising or falling. If the elevation is rising, you will have an uphill climb. If the numbers are getting smaller, you will be traveling downhill on the particular stretch you are examining.

To gain experience with topographical maps you should

get one for an area that you are familiar with and then try to relate the rise and fall of the ground with the contour lines on the map. You should try to calculate the gradient for a few hills on the map and then go out and ride over them to see what the gradient means in terms of actual cycling.

To calculate gradient you will have to relate the topographical map to a road map and draw in the route you plan to take on the topographical map. You can then sight along your route and see how the contour lines are spaced at the particular points you will have to cross. If you want to get accurate about the size of the hills you plan to travel over, you can calculate the gradient by first measuring along the line of travel to see what the distance is between the two points you are dealing with on the map. Find the elevation of the contour lines at either end of the measured stretch and subtract the lowest elevation from the highest elevation (make sure that you are looking at a stretch with a consistent rise or fall of elevation). This will give you the total change in elevation between the two points. If you place the number of feet of rise or fall in elevation over the number of miles along the portion of the route you have just measured, you will have a fraction that will tell you the average change in elevation expressed in feet per mile. This will give you an accurate picture of what type of hill you will be traveling over. You should try this calculation in an area that you are familiar with so that you will have an idea of how large a fraction represents how large or small a hill.

You could spend hours getting technical by calculating the time it takes you to travel certain gradients at certain speeds, or worse yet, the speed you will be able to travel along certain gradients with certain cadences in certain gears. This would certainly become a bit cumbersome and spoil much of the spontaneous enjoyment of cycling. You should, however, be able at least to approximate the type of terrain you will have to cover when planning a trip with your bicycle.

SCALES: Maps are a representation of the surface of the earth and when maps are made, a scale is selected to show distance by making a certain distance on the map equal to a certain distance on the ground. This makes it possible to give a true representation of the relative size of an area. The scale also makes it possible for the reader of a map to calculate distances from one point to another.

There are three different ways of expressing scale. There may be a statement of how many miles on the ground are represented by one inch on the map, such as: two inches (on the map) to the mile (on the ground), or one-half inch to the mile. It may also be expressed by a fraction, such as the ratio of 1:24,000. This means that every unit on the map equals 24,000 units on the ground. One inch on the map in this case would equal 24,000 inches on the ground, or about 2,000 feet. This type of scale is the one used on the topographic maps of the United States. The third way of expressing scale is with a visual or graphic scale. This is a line drawn on the map which is calibrated and marked with the distance on the ground represented by each calibration. This is the scale usually used on road maps.

In choosing the maps you are going to use you should remember to consider the size of the scale. A map with a scale that is closest to a 1:1 representation of the earth's surface will give greater detail than a map that has a scale further away from full scale.

FOLDING MAPS: To reduce the size of your maps and to make them easier to use they should be folded. You can also cut off any margins or excess space to reduce the size, but be sure that you leave the legend and the scale if you are not familiar with them.

To fold a map you should lay it down face-up and, starting at one end, crease the map at two- to three-inch intervals along the vertical plane. Fold these panels into accordian

KNOW THE WAY

type pleats by putting the first panel behind the map and the second over the face of the map, etc. Once you have the map pleated you can make horizontal folds that will reduce the map to a convenient size.

By folding your maps this way you can open them to any spot you need to examine by just unfolding one of the pleats. You do not have to unfold the entire map and then refold it again every time you want to look at it. It will also make it possible for you to read the map easily in a wind or glance at it while pedaling.

CARRYING MAPS: You can carry maps in your pockets or in convenient places in your saddlebags or panniers. Make sure that they are easy to reach because you will probably want to refer to them regularly while on the road. If you want to keep a constant watch on where you are going or what types of gradient lie ahead, you can fasten clips to your handlebars which will hold the maps in place while you are riding.

Chapter 11

Buying a Used Bicycle

If you want to get a good-quality bicycle and save yourself some money at the same time, you should consider buying a used one. It is a risky business, however, and you should have an idea of what to look for when you are shopping around. A bicycle may look bright and shiny and still fall apart before you have ridden more than a few miles. Buying a lemon will leave you with repair bills that will more than use up the money you saved by buying a used bicycle in the first place.

Every aspect of the bicycle should be checked thoroughly before you decide to buy it. If possible, take the bike for a ride. If you cannot take a ride on it, and even if you can, you should literally take the bike apart and check all of its mechanisms thoroughly. A thorough check will save you many problems if conducted before you decide to buy.

Don't be fooled by fancy accessories which will probably be discarded for more practical accouterments once you start riding. Fresh paint is deceiving, and polished chrome is just that! Generally, a bicycle that has been well cared for will have a good appearance, but remember that you cannot judge a bicycle by its trimmings. Bicycles today are precision pieces of machinery and unless they have been cared for properly they will not function properly.

FRAME: The frame should be checked carefully for signs of past damage. Make sure that the frame is straight and has no dents as evidence of accidents or abuse. Check around the joints in the frame to see if there are any ripples in the metal or the paint. If there are, it means that the bike has suffered an accident and the frame may be bent or weakened.

You should know which frames are best for a smooth ride and have sturdy lightweight construction. The frame is actually the suspension system on a bicycle and a frame of heavy metal and poor construction will give you a jostling as you ride. Check the chapter on buying a new bicycle to see which frames are best.

What applies to the frames also applies to the front and rear forks. Make sure that they are straight, aligned, and free of dents. A bicycle frame that has been kept from accidents is going to last much longer than one that has been straightened for the benefit of a prospective buyer, so check closely for signs of damage.

WHEELS: The wheels should be checked to make sure that the rims are straight and free of dents. If your rim is not straight after you buy the bicycle, or if it bends during the first few weeks of riding, it will have to be replaced. It is quite a job to replace a rim so check it out before you buy.

Check the spokes to see what kind of condition they are in. Check the tension to see whether or not the spokes have been kept evenly adjusted. Bad spokes will produce a bad rim. If the spokes are not in good condition, or are not adjusted properly, check the rim thoroughly.

Turn the bicycle upside down and spin the wheels. The eye can catch irregularities with greater ease and accuracy on a turning wheel than on one that is stationary. Check also to see if there is any wobble in the wheel. If there is, you will have to examine the hub closely to see what condition the bearings are in. If tightening the axle nuts or hub casing eliminates the wobble, you are probably safe in assuming that the bearings are good and only a minor adjustment was needed. If there is still a wobble after making these adjustments, you should be prepared to replace the wheel bearings, the hub, or the adjusting cones before you can take the bicycle out on the road.

The wheels should turn freely on the axle. If there are any spots that slow the wheel down appreciably during a single revolution, it means that something is bent and is binding the wheel. If the wheel turns hard, the adjusting cones may be too tight. Adjust the cones and if it still doesn't turn freely there may be frozen wheel bearings or a broken axle inside the hub. When testing the wheels make sure that you do so without the chain. The wheels should turn easily when given a light spin and should come to a gradual stop by themselves.

If the wheels rub against the forks, check carefully to see whether it is the position of the wheel in the fork that is causing the problem. If the wheel is not properly centered, it will only need to be adjusted. If the fork is bent or the rim is bent, it will take more than an adjustment to correct the problem.

You should also check to see how the tires are worn. If the tread is worn unevenly, there is something on the wheel that has not been kept properly aligned. The rims may be bent or the brakes may not be correctly adjusted, so you should give the wheel a good look if the tire is worn unevenly.

BRAKES: If the bicycle has a coaster brake you should check to see whether the brake arm is tight, and then test the brake on an actual ride. The brake should have enough braking power to make the rear wheel skid on dry pavement. The brake should not interfere with the movement of the wheel once it is released. If it does, there is something wrong and the bicycle should be passed up for one in better condition. Brakes are important to your safety so be sure to test them well.

With caliper hand brakes you should check to see how the brake blocks are worn. If they are worn unevenly, they have not been adjusted properly and have been grabbing the wheel irregularly. When the brake lever is released the brake blocks should return to their original position, clear of the wheel rim. They should not rub on the rim while the bicycle is in motion. Test front and rear hand brakes separately to make sure that there is no shaking in the bicycle when the brakes are applied. The brakes should grab evenly and firmly.

GEARS: With three-speed gears you will have to make sure that the cable works smoothly. If it does not engage the gears properly there are probably kinks in the cable and it will have to be replaced. If the gears are not engaging properly or are not staying engaged, you should try adjusting the gear-cable tension to see if that will solve the problem (see the chapter on repairs). If the gears are still slipping even after you have made the adjustment on the cable, the clutch would have to be replaced and the bicycle should be passed up. If you feel anything unusual when changing gears, something is probably wrong. Even if you can't quite put your finger on what doesn't feel right, trust your judgment. If gears do not shift and engage smoothly, the parts are probably worn and you will end up replacing them sooner or later.

On ten-speed derailleur bicycles you should check for any signs of abuse to the gear-changing mechanism. A bent or damaged derailleur will show signs of wear on the parts because the chain will not have been riding properly in the mechanism. Check to make sure there are no marks on the inside of the derailleur cage. Also look at the sprockets to see if they are worn evenly. If they show evidence of uneven wear, the bicycle has been operating without having been adjusted properly and there will probably be wear on all derailleur parts and the chain. If the derailleur is bent considerably, you will probably have to replace the unit to make sure that there are no signs of damage. Take the bicycle out for a ride and make sure that the derailleur changes smoothly through all the gears and there is no slipping from one gear to another. Listen carefully for any unusual noises that will give you a clue as to the condition of the unit.

Check the alignment of the sprockets with relation to the bicycle and to one another. If there are any bent sprockets, they will have to be replaced. You should also check to see if the rear-sprocket cluster and the front-chain wheels are aligned with one another. Check the adjustment of the derailleur and make sure that both low- and high-gear adjustments are accurate. If the derailleur is not adjusted correctly, you will have to make these adjustments yourself if you buy the bicycle. You will also have to take the consequences of someone else's neglect. A derailleur that has been kept in proper alignment and adjustment and free of accidents, will last much longer than one that has been neglected or abused.

CHAIN: Carefully examine the chain for uneven wear. Check also to make sure that it fits snugly and neatly on the sprockets. If there are damaged links in the chain they will not fit well into the teeth of the sprockets and you can spot quickly how many you will have to replace. Check to make sure that the chain has been well greased and that there are no rust spots. If the chain is rusted, it will have to be replaced—and it has already damaged the other parts of the bicycle that it has come in contact with when in operation.

PEDALS: The pedals should turn freely without binding. Check to see if they are bent. If they are, you will have to replace them. It is very annoying to have a pedal that does not keep your foot flat in relation to the frame of the bicycle. Riding with damaged pedals will greatly reduce your efficiency and greatly increase the amount of fatigue on your feet. You should also make sure that there is no side play in the pedals. Check the threads on the pedal to make sure there are no signs of stripping. A pedal can be forced into place for a short period of time even if the threads are stripped, but it will eventually fall out of its proper position.

The entire front-sprocket assembly should turn without any sign of binding or wobble. Take the chain off and give the pedals a light spin. The unit should come to a stop slowly and there should be no signs of uneven turning. Make sure that the crank is not bent in any way; this will force you to pedal unevenly when you ride. Trying to straighten the crank may result in damage to the crank hanger, so the bicycle you purchase should have cranks that are not damaged in any way.

GENERAL CHECK: You should check a prospective bicycle from front to rear for any missing or damaged bolts. If the bolts are missing, check to see if there is damage to other parts because of it. The same holds true for bolts that are loose or not fitted properly. If the bolts are not in place, there is a good possibility that whoever owns the bicycle has been riding it improperly.

Remember that there are any number of minor adjustments and repairs that you can make yourself to put a basically good bicycle into top running condition. If the bicycle has many of the features that you want, and the price is right, it may be worth your while to purchase it and then make a slight overhaul to give yourself a fine machine. It should be kept in mind, however, that a bicycle that has been well cared for will last longer and give you far less headaches in the long run.

You may have finally decided which bicycle it is you want to buy and have purchased it, but you are not yet ready to take that long-awaited spin around the neighborhood to show off your new acquisition. Before you start to ride your newly purchased bicycle, you should take it apart completely. You should clean and regrease all the bearings. You should grease the chain and make sure that all the parts of your wheel and hub assemblies are in good condition and adjusted properly. Replace any worn parts before they do any damage to other parts of the bicycle. If one part is allowed to go unreplaced, you may be faced with the problem of replacing much more in the future. When buying a used bicycle you should take into consideration the fact that you will have to spend a little time and money beyond the purchase price of the bicycle and the effort of locating one that you like. To have a good machine you will have to put in a little work.

When you put your bicycle back together make sure that all your wheels and gear units are properly in line. You will cause damage to your gears and rims if your wheels and sprockets are not lined up correctly. As a final check, make sure that all bolts are firmly in place and that none are worn. It is much easier to prevent disaster than to deal with it once it has struck.

With your bicycle thoroughly cleaned, greased, and properly adjusted, you can take it out and enjoy the same riding pleasure as those who have just spent far more on a brand-new machine.

WHERE TO LOOK: There are two places where a used bicycle can be bought: One is a bicycle shop that takes trade-ins on new bicycles. Most bicycle shops will sell used bicycles as a part of their regular business. The other place is from a private party who is parting with his.

If you go to a bicycle shop, you are liable to have a greater selection from which to choose. Most shops carry more than one bicycle and, if you shop around at a number of them, you can easily look at a staggering number in only a few hours. If you want to buy from another person you will only be able to see one bicycle at a time and may have to travel great distances to look at very many of them. You can save yourself time if you ask some pertinent questions over the telephone; this will eliminate wild goose chases, but you will still have to cover a lot of territory to find the right bicycle.

One advantage that you will have if you buy from a private party is that you will stand a better chance of getting more for your money. Sometimes people have to sell items because they need the money quickly and they are willing to sell them at a loss. Store owners are involved in making a profit and have to sell their merchandise on that basis. You won't necessarily get a bad deal from a bicycle shop, but you won't necessarily get a good one, either.

As far as the condition of the bicycle you buy goes, a bicycle shop will probably have already done all of the overhauling that you would have to do yourself if you bought your bicycle from a private party. One thing that you should keep in mind, however, is that the bicycle dealers will be somewhat more reluctant to replace worn parts than you will if you do the work yourself. You should tear your bicycle apart and check it thoroughly even if you buy it from a dealer. Another problem with buying from a bicycle shop is the fact that it is harder to tell how well the bicycle was treated by its former owner. Once many of the problems have already been touched up and adjusted you may not know whether the person who had the bicycle before you was careful with it or whether he abused it.

BUYING A USED BICYCLE

To find bicycle dealers, your best bet is to look in the yellow pages of the phone book. Advertising in bicycle magazines may also be of help if you live in a large city and the shops are likely to advertise in your area. Your local chamber of commerce may also be able to help supply information as to where you can find a reputable dealer. Ask the local cycling organization if they can recommend a good place to buy used bicycles or if any of their members are trying to sell theirs. Shop around and take your time. The time you spend looking will be more than made up for by the money you may save and the time you will spend making repairs if you don't.

Chapter 12

Repair Guide

Anyone who owns his own bicycle should be able to make most of the basic repairs necessary to keep it rolling. With the high cost of repairing anything these days, if most of your repairs can be made at home you will save yourself a substantial amount of money over the years. Aside from the monetary aspect, you can be sure that your bicycle has been worked on properly if you do the work yourself. In many cases you can spend a small fortune having your bicycle repaired by a supposed expert and still not have it returned in good running condition. If you plan to do any traveling with your bicycle, it is best to have some knowledge of repairs so you will be able to fix your bicycle while on the road. You can't always depend on the luxury of a repair shop because your bicycle will not always break down in front of one. If you are able to cope with whatever problems you may encounter on the road, it will save you many a long walk.

For those repairs that you cannot make yourself, you will need a good mechanic. They are not easy to find, but they do exist so you should spend some time looking. With a basic knowledge of how your bicycle operates and what can go wrong with it you will be able to hold your own in the face of bicycle repair double-talk. Ask a few questions from the person you are considering and see what kind of answers you get. If you know your bicycle, you will be able to judge the knowledge and honesty of the person who will be working on it.

If you should need any repair work done that you can't do yourself, it would be worth a trip to some local bicycle club or organization. They can recommend a good local mechanic or maybe even give you some help that will enable you to make the repair yourself, after all. People who are actively involved in cycling know their bicycles and are usually willing to pass on their knowledge to anyone who shows an interest in learning.

WHAT TO FIX: Depending on your ability with mechanical contraptions, there are some things on a bicycle that it may be better to leave to a good bicycle repairman. If you are mechanically inclined and able to take things apart without forgetting how to put them back together again, there is very little on a bicycle that you won't be able to deal with. It may take a little time and more than a little patience, but it is not beyond the realm of possibility.

This may sound a bit strange and ironic, but the higher quality derailleur bicycles are less complicated than the three- or five-speed varieties that use a multispeed and coaster brake hub assembly. The multifunctioning of the multispeed hub makes it necessary for it to have a great number of parts, and disassembly will require many special tools. These units are better left to an experienced mechanic with the proper tools.

Derailleur gear units are not as complicated as multispeed rear hubs and there is also less that can go wrong with them. Proper adjustment and a little knowledge of how the derailleur works should keep your gearing repairs at home. Even if you have no mechanical inclinations, you should at least know how to align your derailleur mechanism to get the smoothest operation. Fine tuning on a derailleur is a personalized art and anyone who rides a bicycle equipped with a derailleur unit should be able to master this art satisfactorily.

Hand brakes, pedals, flat tires, handlebars, and normal hub assemblies are not particularly complicated and should present very few problems in maintenance and repair. Adjustment and replacement of minor parts can easily be done with very little technical knowledge and a few tools at home.

FLAT TIRES: Everyone who rides a bicycle will sooner or later experience a flat tire. Repairing flat tires is easy and inexpensive. You will need a repair kit and, with clincher tires, a couple of simple tools. If you have tubular racing tires, you should be careful to use only ultrathin patches. If you get a patch that is too thick, it will produce a bulge in your tire once you have made the repair. This can be annoying at best since it is liable to thump along as you ride, and at worst can cause damage to your tire.

If you have a slow leak, you should always check the valve before you try to find the leak in the tube. A loose or worn valve core will let air escape slowly, in which case it needs only to be tightened or replaced to remedy the loss of air. To check your valve take a mixture of soap and water (liquid dishwashing soap works best) and with the dust cap removed place the mixture in the valve so that it covers the opening. If a bubble forms in the valve, you should tighten the valve core with a valve tool. Test again for leakage. If you still get a bubble, you will have to replace the valve core.

Clincher Tires: To check a tube for damage you will first have to remove the tire from the rim. With clincher tires this will require two flat-edge screwdrivers or tire levers.

Remove the wheel from the fork and check the tire for signs of damage. If you find a spot that looks as if it may have caused the flat, you will not have to remove the entire tube to patch it.

Lay the wheel on its side and insert one tire lever carefully between the tire and the rim. You have to make sure when removing the tire that you don't puncture the tube. Once the lever is in place you should pry the tire over the rim by pushing down on the lever. Leave this lever in place and insert the second lever about 6 inches to either side of the first. With the second lever pry another section of the tire over the rim. Continue this process around the rim, leaving the original lever in place to keep the tire from slipping back into place.

When you have one side of the tire freed from the rim, you can remove the tube and the other side of the tire by hand. To find the leak you should inflate the tire and rotate it slowly near your ear. You should be able to hear a hissing sound at the site of the puncture. If the leak is too small to be heard, you can immerse the tube in a tub of water and bubbles will appear at the site of the puncture.

Once you have found the leak, mark it with a piece of chalk. Next take a piece of sandpaper or the metal abrader that comes with your repair kit and roughen the surface of the tube where you have marked the leak. This will help to ensure a good seal when you place the patch on. Put some rubber cement around the puncture over an area that roughly conforms to the size of the patch you are going to use. When the cement has dried to a sticky surface, carefully pull the backing off the patch. Try not to touch the side of the patch that will be applied to the surface of the tube. Any grease from your fingers will prevent your making a good seal. Put the patch on the tube and press it firmly in place. Give the patch a chance to dry and then dust the area with talcum powder. This will keep any excess glue from sticking to the inside of the tire when you replace the tube.

To replace the tube and tire, inflate the tube slightly to give it some shape and tuck it into the tire. Put the valve stem into the valve hole on the rim. Make sure that the valve is straight and remains straight once you have the tire back in place. If the tire pulls the valve in either direction it will be damaged against the rim. Once the valve is in place you can push the tire over the rim with your hands. Be careful to avoid pinching the tube between the tire and the rim; if you do you could have to start the process all over again or replace the tube.

Tubular Racing Tires: Tubular racing tires are a bit more difficult to patch than clincher tires because the tube is sewn into the tire. These tires are called "sew ups" because that is exactly what you will have to do to repair the tire.

Remove the wheel from the fork and the tire from the rim. The tire is cemented in so you will have to apply a bit of pressure to roll it off the rim. Start on the side opposite the valve to prevent damage to it. Reinflate the tire and submerge it, a bit at a time, in a tub of water. Do not be alarmed if some air escapes from around the valve. This is normal and is not the cause of your flat tire. When you have found the leak, mark the tire with a piece of chalk.

You will now have to cut along the stitching in the tire to expose the tube. Separate the rim tape from the casing for approximately 3 inches on either side of the puncture (A).

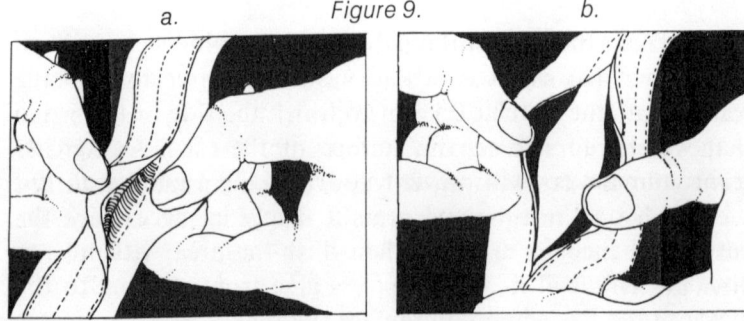

Figure 9.

Repairing Tubulars

The stitching will then be exposed. Mark a few lines across the stitching, about an inch apart, to aid realignment when you resew the tire. Carefully cut along the stitches approximately 2½ inches on either side of the puncture. Do not cut down into the stitches. Get underneath and cut in an upward direction. This will keep you from cutting the tire or the tube. Remove the inside-tube protecting tape and the tube will be exposed (B).

Repair the tube in the same manner described for patching the tubes on clincher tires. Be sure to use ultrathin patches. Remember to coat the patch with talcum powder—this is even more important with tubulars.

With the needle and thread in your repair kit, carefully restitch the tire using the same holes that were used for the original stitches. Tie a knot in the end of the thread and start your stitching so that it overlaps the original stitching that was left intact. A simple overhand stitch will be sufficient to hold the tube in place. Be careful not to puncture the tube with your needle when you are sewing the tire. When you have finished, put rubber cement over the stitching and on the base tape. When the cement is dry, replace the base tape so that it lies flat and is free of wrinkles.

To put the repaired tire back on the rim you will need either rim cement or rim tape. This is necessary since tubulars that are not held firmly in place on the rim may slip off when going around turns. Even if they stay on there is liable to be a certain amount of roll in the tire which can cause damage. Remove all old rim cement before applying a fresh coat. If this is allowed to build up it will produce an uneven surface for the tire to ride on. Also make sure that no spokes are protruding through the rim. If they are, you will have to file them down.

When you have coated the rim with rim cement or rim tape, place the valve in the valve hole with both hands and start to fit the tire onto the rim. Work from the top to the bottom of the wheel on either side. When you have reached the bottom of the wheel, you should be able to work the last few inches onto the rim with your thumbs. Once you have the tire in place, inflate slightly and wait for the rim cement to dry. When it is dry you can inflate to full pressure.

COASTER BRAKES: If cared for properly a coaster brake should last for the life of the bicycle. The brake and hub assembly should be lubricated once a month to keep the parts from becoming worn and needing replacement. If the bicycle does not coast freely or the brake drags on the wheel when the wheel is turning, you probably need oil or grease in the brake unit. Improper lubrication also causes the brakes to grab or make a squealing noise when applied. About once a year you should take your bicycle to a bicycle shop and have the brake assembly dismantled, cleaned, and regreased. If you wish to do this yourself, you should write to the manufacturer and request assembly and disassembly instructions to guide you.

If the coaster brake locks and does not allow the wheel to move in either direction, you will have to readjust the adjusting cone. Loosen the axle nuts and turn the cone outward. If the cone is badly worn it should be replaced. Retighten the axle nuts and test ride. If this does not solve the problem, there is internal damage and the unit should be taken to a repair shop.

The brake clip, which is attached to either the frame or the rear fork, is the anchor on which the coaster brake stops the wheel. This bracket should be checked regularly to make sure that it is not worn and that it is firmly in place. If the brake arm is loose, it should be turned forward. Once it is tight it should be held in place by the bracket. If the brake does not engage properly, check to make sure that the brake arm is not loose. If the brakes do not engage at all, check to make sure that the bracket has not broken and allowed the brake arm to turn freely.

HAND BRAKES: Caliper or hand brakes need constant adjustment. This type of brake slows the wheel by applying friction to both sides of the rim with small rubber pads. Since these pads must rub against the rim, they are constantly decreasing in size. The pads should be kept approximately 1/8 inch from the rim, so as they wear down you will have to readjust the caliper brake arms.

To adjust caliper brakes you first have to make sure that the brake shoe lines up with the rim properly. They should make contact parallel to the rim, and if they don't, you will have to loosen the nut that holds the brake shoe in place and adjust the shoe until it is in the proper position with respect to the rim. Then tighten the locknut.

To adjust the distance from the brake pad to the rim you will have to loosen the locknut that holds the cable in place and turn the cable adjusting barrel until the brake pad is 1/8 inch away from the rim. If there is too much slack in the cable to make the adjustment, you will have to loosen the cable anchor bolt and pull the cable through about 1/4 inch. Be careful not to let the cable slip out of the anchor hole. If it does you will be hard-pressed to fit the frayed cable end back into the hole and will probably have to replace the

REPAIR GUIDE

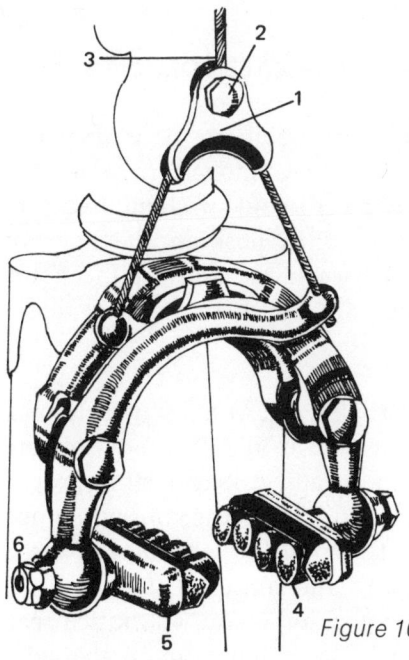

Center-pull Brake

1. Cable anchor
2. Cable anchor nut and bolt
3. Brake cable
4. Brake pad
5. Brake block
6. Brake block adjusting and holding cut

Figure 10.

entire cable with a new one. Once you have taken up the slack in the brake cable, you can again adjust the adjusting barrel until the brake pad is the proper distance away from the rim.

Eventually your brake pads will wear all the way down and will have to be replaced. Even if you do not ride enough to wear the pads down, they deteriorate with age and the rubber loses its elasticity. If your brake pads are hard and have no spring left in them, they should be replaced. To replace a brake pad you have only to slip the old pad from the brake block and replace it with a new one. Once in a while, it would be a good idea to replace the entire brake pad and block assembly. This does not cost much more than replacing the brake pad by itself and it will keep your brakes functioning properly. When replacing the brake block remember to have the closed metal end of the brake block facing the front of the bicycle. If you get them turned around your brake pad will slide out of the brake block when the brakes are applied.

If your brake arms do not release freely or if they rub against one another when the brake is applied, they may be bent. If the brake arms are not made out of aluminum, you can carefully bend them back into position. If they are aluminum, you can file in between the arms at the point where they are making contact until they move independently of one another.

ADJUSTING STURMEY-ARCHER GEARS: If you have a Sturmey-Archer multispeed rear hub and it is not shifting properly, you may only need to adjust it to restore proper functioning. To adjust a Sturmey-Archer gear you should put the gear shift in the number two position (the number three position on five-speed units), and unscrew the locknut located on the cable near the rear hub. You will notice that there is a nut on the axle with a window cut in the side. Inside this window you will find an indicator rod. This indicator rod should be exactly level with the end of the rear axle, which you will also be able to see in the window. Adjust the cable until the axle and indicator rod are aligned and then retighten the locknut. If you need more adjustment than can be made with the cable adjustment, unscrew the nut and bolt which holds the cable on the top tube. You can then adjust the cable length, retighten the nut and bolt, and make the needed adjustments with the method described above.

There should be no need to adjust the gear shift at all. If it is bent or damaged it should be replaced.

DERAILLEUR GEARS: The most common cause of derailleur failure is improper adjustment. If the unit is not changing gears correctly and smoothly, something is more than likely out of alignment. The derailleur is one of the most sophisticated parts of your bicycle, and you must make precision adjustments if you are to minimize chain wear and get the smoothest possible gear changes.

There are four different parts which carry the chain on a derailleur-equipped bicycle: the front chainwheel, the rear sprocket cluster, and front and rear derailleur mechanisms. Each of these parts must be aligned with one another properly.

The front chainwheel and the rear sprocket cluster must be aligned with one another. If you sight down a line from the

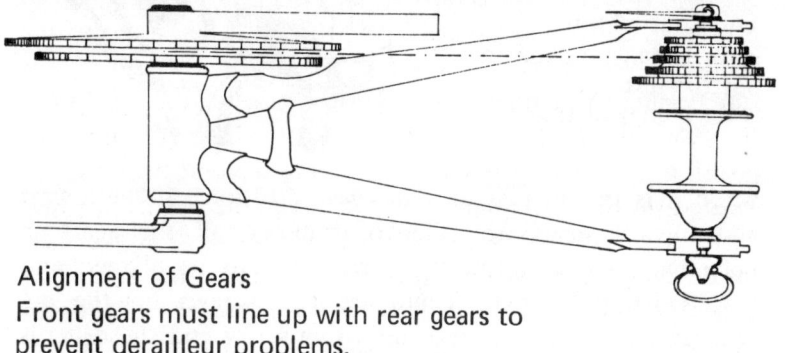

Alignment of Gears
Front gears must line up with rear gears to prevent derailleur problems.
Figure 11.

middle sprocket of the rear cluster to the front chainwheel, the sprocket should be aligned with the space between the two sprockets on the chainwheel. If the sprockets are not lined up properly, the chain will not ride evenly on them through all the gears.

Every make of derailleur has different screws for adjusting the positions of the front and rear derailleur mechanisms. The derailleur chain cages must be adjusted for both the high gear and the low gear. The purpose of the cage is to move the chain from one sprocket to another and to keep the chain riding correctly on the sprockets once it is in gear. To adjust the cage you have to align the chainwheels with the sprockets

Simplex "Prestige"
Derailleur Adjustment

Top knurled nut
is for large-gear chain;
bottom nut
is for high-gear travel.

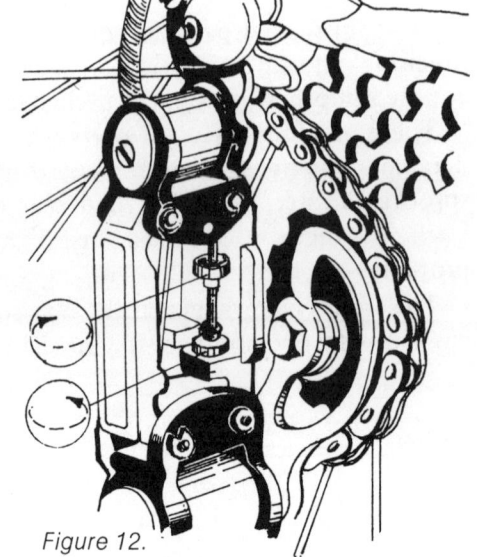
Figure 12.

while it is in the two extreme gear positions. If the lowest and highest gears are aligned properly, all the gears in between, barring sprocket damage, should be aligned and your shifting smooth. There are two screws on the derailleur: one is the low-gear adjusting screw and the other is the high-gear adjusting screw. You should know where these two screws are located on your particular derailleur mechanism.

The low-gear adjustment is important. If not adjusted properly, the chain may slip off the large sprocket and damage your spokes. To adjust the low gear, place the chain on the small front sprocket and the largest rear sprocket. The low-gear adjusting screw should then be turned until the chainwheels line up with the sprocket. You should test this adjustment by turning the pedals while in low gear and watching to see if the chain makes any attempt to ride off the sprocket. If it does not stay on the sprocket evenly, it should be readjusted.

The same procedure should be performed for the high

REPAIR GUIDE

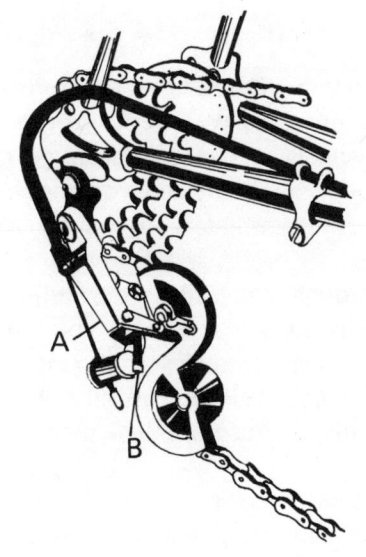

Huret "Allvit" Derailleur
and Adjustments
for High Speed (A)
and Low Speed (B)

Figure 13.

gear. Put the chain on the large front sprocket and the smallest rear sprocket and adjust the high-gear adjustment screw until the chain rides properly.

If you cannot get the chain to ride properly when adjusting the chain cage, there may be something else out of line or your derailleur may be bent. If the derailleur is bent and the chainwheels do not carry the chain correctly, you can straighten it by forcing it gently back into position. Do not try to hit it with a hammer. Steady firm pressure should be applied.

If your chain slips while the bicycle is in gear, your chain tension may need adjusting. Once again, this adjustment is different for different brands of derailleurs, so you should know how to adjust your own chain tension on your own bicycle. If you have correct chain tension and it still slips, your sprockets may be worn and they should be checked. If they are, they should be replaced. Your chain may also be the cause of the problem. If it is badly worn, it will not fit onto the sprockets and will slip off while riding.

If the chain slips off the sprockets even after all the proper adjustments have been made, you may have a bent sprocket. If this happens when the bicycle is in one particular gear, then it probably is due to a bent sprocket, and you should check to see. If you find a bent sprocket, you can try to straighten it or replace it.

If your gears change while riding, you will have to adjust the gear-shift control lever. If the lever is too loose you will find the gears changing on their own. Your levers should be tight enough to feel snug, but you should be careful not to tighten them to the point that shifting becomes difficult.

WHEELS: If your wheel wobbles, there are many possible causes to investigate. The wheel may only be loose, in which case you should tighten the axle nuts on both sides of the wheel. If the wheel still wobbles, your cones may not be adjusted properly. Remove the wheel and look at the cones carefully. You will notice that one is smooth and the other is notched for a wrench. Place a wrench, generally 1/2 inch or 9/16 inch, over the notched end and turn clockwise until there is no play in the hub. If the hub is worn you should replace it.

Another possible cause of a wobbly wheel is worn wheel bearings. If you suspect that the bearings are worn, you should replace them. If the hub and wheel bearings wear out frequently, you should check to see if the axle is bent. If it is bent it should be replaced.

If the wheel does not turn at all, or if it turns sluggishly, it may be rubbing against the fork. Check the wheel alignment and if this is not the problem, make sure the cones aren't too tight. Loosen the cones, and if that does not solve the problem, check the wheel bearings to see if they may be frozen. Grease the bearings, or, if they are worn badly, replace them. You may also have a broken axle, so this should be checked if no other remedy works. If the axle doesn't turn properly it should be replaced.

Chapter 13

Gearing

One of the most important advances in the development of the bicycle was the introduction of gearing. Before gearing was available to the cyclist he had to huff and puff over hills with no help from his bicycle at all. Having a selection of gears enables the cyclist to maintain a steady rhythm on his pedals practically independent of the grade over which he is traveling. If you do not have multiple gears on your bicycle, you will want to, sooner or later. To cycle effectively, a change of gear is essential. To use the gears you have effectively, and to aid you in selecting the gears you will want to have, you should have an understanding of the basic principles of gearing.

GEAR PRINCIPLE: All bicycles have at least two sprockets, one in the front and one in the rear. The front sprocket is turned by the pedals and it, in turn, spins the rear sprocket. If the number of teeth on the sprockets is the same, the sprockets will revolve in unison. This means that for every turn you apply to the front sprocket there will be a concomitant turn in the rear sprocket, consequently, one revolution of the rear wheel.

Sprockets vary in the number of teeth they have, but for the sake of the explanation, let's assume that the front sprocket of a bicycle has 40 teeth and the rear sprockets have 20 teeth, 10 teeth, and 5 teeth. If you are riding this bicycle in the highest gear (the chain is on the rear sprocket with 5 teeth), the rear wheel will turn 8 times with every revolution of the pedals. This means that you will move along the ground a distance of 8 times the circumference of the wheel.

Now suppose that you are traveling in this gear and you approach a steep hill. If you stay in high gear, it will require the application of more energy on the pedals to keep up the spin against the gradient of the hill. It will be more work to get the wheel to turn 8 times with every revolution of the pedals. If, however, you change your gear by sliding the chain off the 5-tooth sprocket and onto the sprocket with 10 teeth, you will only be turning the rear wheel 4 times with every revolution of the pedals. This cuts in half the amount of energy required to turn the pedal. You will only travel half as far with every revolution of the pedals as when you were riding in high gear. This will, of course, slow you down, but you will be able to keep practically the same pedal spin in spite of the effect of gravity you are working against. You will be taking the hill in smaller increments and each increment will be easier to travel.

If we draw an analogy this may be easier to understand. It

is the same as trying to lift 200 pounds of brick from the ground to a platform 6 feet off the ground. If you tried to lift the entire load at once, it would require a great deal of effort and the drain of energy on your body would be great. If you lift the bricks 10 pounds at a time, you will still have performed the same amount of work, but it will take you a little longer and your body will not notice the effort.

If the gear you have selected is not sufficient to carry you over the hill, you can again change gears. This time you will slip the chain onto the sprocket that has 20 teeth. You will again cut the amount of energy it takes to turn the pedals in half. Again you will only move the bicycle half the distance with every turn of the pedals, making the hill easier to climb by breaking it down into smaller increments which are easier to handle.

Once you are over the top of the hill you will have gravity working for you instead of against you. If you keep the bicycle in low gear, your pedals will turn once with every two revolutions of the rear wheel. Since you will gain speed on the downhill run, you will be hard-pressed to keep up with your pedals. It would be even harder to apply pressure to them. If you switch back into your highest gear, your pedals will make one revolution for every eight turns of the rear wheel. Since you have to turn your pedals less frequently with every turn of the wheel, you will be able to add extra speed to that already given to you by the force of gravity, rather than having just to keep up with it.

Thus, by changing gears you can maintain a relatively even spin on your pedals regardless of whether you are going uphill or down. With a good steady pedal spin you can cover much longer distances with less fatigue than if you had to pump harder on your uphill runs.

Those who have three- or five-speed bicycles should not be alarmed by the fact that they only have two sprockets and can still change gears. On multispeed hubs the gearing is done on the inside of the wheel hub which contains its own system of gear ratios.

SELECTING GEARS: The gear ratios you will have to choose from will depend on the bicycle you have and what size the sprockets are on the chainwheel and rear sprocket cluster. Different bicycles come with different gear ranges. If the gear ratios are varied from one to another in large increments, you will have a wide range of gearing possibilities.

The greater the difference between the largest and smallest rear sprockets, the easier your bicycle will be to pedal. Many racing cyclists and avid enthusiasts prefer a closer gear-ratio range than the average cyclist. This enables them to maintain a good speed, but it also requires a greater amount of effort and stamina. With a close range of gear ratios, the cyclist will not notice as much of a difference in changing from one gear to the next than if he were riding a bicycle with a wider range of gear ratios.

The bicycle of the average cyclist should have sprockets with a range of approximately 14 to 28 teeth on the rear cluster and sprockets of 39 and 50 teeth on the front chainwheel. This will give you incremental differences of 4 teeth on the rear sprockets and 11 teeth on the chainwheel. This range should be wide enough for the average cyclist. If you want a closer range, be prepared to do more work.

GEAR RATIOS AND CADENCE: If you want a better understanding of exactly which gears you have on your bicycle and what they can do, you should be able to calculate gear ratios and cadence. This will translate the number of teeth you have on your sprockets into a chart which tells you how far and how fast you will be able to travel in every gear.

Since distance traveled along the ground with each revolution of the wheel will depend on the wheel size, you

GEARING

will have to know what size wheels you have on your bicycle. For the sake of calculation I will use a 26-inch wheel in calculating gear ratios. To find out how far you will travel with every revolution of the pedals, you should multiply the wheel circumference by the fraction formed when you place the number of teeth on the front sprocket in the numerator and the number of teeth on the rear sprocket in the denominator. In other words, no. of teeth in front sprocket ÷ no. of teeth in rear sprocket x wheel size = distance traveled with each revolution of the pedal. If you have a front sprocket of 50 teeth, a rear sprocket of 24 teeth, and a wheel size of 26 inches, the distance traveled with every revolution of the pedals would be, 50 ÷ 24 x 26 or 54.2 inches.

To mold this information into a more practical form, you should also figure out the cadence for each of your gears. Cadence is the speed at which you will be traveling if you turn your crank a certain number of revolutions per minute in a certain gear.

The average cyclist should pedal somewhere between 55 and 85 revolutions per minute. This pedal spin has been shown to be the most efficient. You should know or be able to estimate your average spin by counting the turns on your crank through 15 seconds and then multiplying that number by four. You may want to try different calculations for different sets of circumstances and then calculate the speed you will be able to travel in different gears at these spins. This will give you a fair idea of what your gearing and pedaling capabilities and possibilities are.

SHIFTING GEARS: If you have a multispeed hub, there will be no problem in shifting gears, but if you have never ridden a ten-speed derailleur bicycle, you will have to learn. Improper shifting can damage the derailleur shifting mechanism, the sprockets, and the chain.

When shifting the derailleur, the cyclist has to maintain his speed and pedal revolutions. There should be very little, if any, pressure exerted on the pedals during the shift. In shifting to lower gears when approaching hills this means that you will have to judge exactly how much speed you are going to lose before the chain is positioned. You have to have enough momentum to make the shift without applying pressure to the pedals, so you will have to gain that momentum in advance.

Without applying pressure to the pedals, you should keep them revolving at the same speed that you set before starting to make the shift. Any backward motion on the pedals could cause damage to the derailleur shifting mechanism and could also stretch or bend the chain.

You should make the shift as quickly as possible without forcing the lever. If the gear will not shift, you do not have sufficient speed and will have to remain in the same gear until you can pedal back to the correct speed. If you are on a hill and have not judged properly, you may not be able to regain the needed momentum and you should walk your bicycle up the hill or stay in the gear you are already in and just struggle. It is better to work a little more or suffer a bit of humiliation than to damage your derailleur.

After you have made your shift, if you hear any sound of rubbing or clatter from your derailleur, the shifting cage is not properly aligned with the sprocket. Adjust the lever forward and backward until the chain rides noiselessly. If that does not solve the problem, you should check the alignment and adjustment of the derailleur shifting mechanisms to see that they are in the proper position. You should also check to make sure that the front and rear sprockets are aligned properly.

Chapter 14

Racing and Endurance Contests

Many people take their bicycles seriously by testing their wits and abilities against other riders in bicycle competition. Bicycle racing is an exciting sport and it is quickly regaining the popularity it once enjoyed in this country. The lack of suitable tracks and public recognition have made it harder for the cyclists in the United States than for their counterparts in Europe where bicycle racing is a highly honored sport and the top cyclists enjoy much public recognition for their accomplishments. The enthusiasm for bicycle racing is much greater in Europe than in this country, but the popularity gap is closing more and more every year as people discover the thrill of watching and participating in this exciting sport.

There are many different types of bicycle races presided

over by the Amateur Bicycle League of America, but they all fall into two general categories: road racing and track racing. As the names imply, the difference lies in the type of course used during the race. This also brings about differences in equipment and technique. Bicycles are specifically designed for either track or road racing and although there is much similarity in the technique used, there is also a degree of difference which makes the two sports less related than might be expected.

TRACK RACING: Track racing is conducted on specifically designed oval tracks. Since there are only a few of these in the country, in many cases, automobile racing tracks or running tracks have had to be used as substitutes. Track racing involves a great deal of skill, ingenuity, and endurance on the part of the participants, and is an exciting sport for the spectator as well, since he can watch all the action from one convenient spot.

The bicycle used by track racers is specifically designed to have the least amount of weight and the highest possible speed. It has a fixed hub and no brakes. This is not exactly the bicycle you would choose if you wanted to ride around in the country. Every bit of extra weight has been stripped off to produce a machine that is far lighter than those used for touring or even road racing. The frame has a shorter wheelbase and the least possible clearance under the fork crown. The tires are extremely lightweight (they only weigh between 5 and 8 ounces) and would not last long on the open road. The rims are much thinner than on road-racing bicycles. Since the track racer does not have to worry about riding over uneven road surfaces, he can afford to take off the extra weight that comes with tires that are less prone to punctures.

Sprint racing is one of the finest events in cycling. It involves two or three riders on a track matched against one another over a defined distance. It takes a great deal of strategy and speed to beat another rider outright. In races

RACING AND ENDURANCE CONTESTS

involving more riders and covering longer distances, other factors than individual ability enter in to determine the winner of the race. In sprint racing you have a one on one situation, and the spirit of competition is high.

Pursuit track racing is a bit different than sprint racing. In pursuit races, the riders start on opposite sides of the track, either individually or in teams, and each rider tries to catch the rider or riders on the opposite side. They do not actually succeed in catching one another, but by logging the best time for the distance a rider can win the race. This type of racing necessitates a different kind of strategy from that of most cycle races. Since the contestants are nowhere near one another, they are not able to outsmart their opponents as easily as in most races. To win this race, a cyclist has to have the endurance and speed to turn in a faster time. Although there is still strategy involved, as there is in any race, a pursuit race is more a test of speed.

Scratch races are the counterparts of the massed-start races in road racing. All the competitors start from the starting line at the same time, and the first cyclist to cross the finish line is the winner of the race.

Point-to-point races are not won by crossing the finish line ahead of the pack. A specific number of laps define the length of the course and sprints are marked at each lap or half-lap. Points are decided by the first one, two, or three men to cross the sprint line on each lap, and the rider with the most points at the end of the race is the winner. This is an exciting race since it combines the thrill of the finish line with the subtleties of good field maneuvering.

Devil-take-the-hindmost races are not as common as the other track races. In this race the last man over the line on each lap is eliminated from the race. This produces a nice change from the races in which most of the attention is focused on the front of the pack. When there are only two racers left on the last lap, the first one over the finish line wins the race.

ROAD RACING: Road racing makes use of the roads which are already in existence for its courses. This makes road racing easier to set up, since most areas cannot obtain a suitable track to conduct track races and the road race can be held in any community that has a lightly traveled road.

Since road racing requires the ability to stop the bicycle in cases of emergency or for any normal road hazard, road racing bicycles have brakes. Roads are not usually as level as a well-made track, and so they also require a selection of gears which will enable the cyclist to climb hills easily and gain maximum speed while traveling downhill. As you may have guessed by now, the road-racing bicycle is not very much different from the average touring bicycle. It is lighter and far more specialized to obtain the highest possible speeds on the road, but it has the derailleur mechanism and brakes that typify most bicycles built for use on the road.

If you are interested in racing and already have a ten-speed bicycle, it would not take much to convert it to a road-racing machine. These races are better suited to the novice racer because they are more common and involve less in specialized equipment and training. Road racing is a good opportunity for anyone to test his stamina and cycling ability against that of other cyclists. Racing does involve a great deal of hard work and hours of rugged training, but anyone with the ability and desire to race will find that his time is well spent.

Time-trial racing pits the cyclist against the clock rather than against another cyclist. Riders are started separately, spaced about a minute apart, and the rider with the best time over the entire course wins the race. Time trials are usually held very early on Sunday mornings since public roads must be used and traffic is lightest at this time; so you will have to rise early if you want to participate or watch. Time trials usually cover distances that range from ten to a hundred miles.

One variation of the time trial is the hill climb. As the name implies, the cyclist must climb a hill, and the one with

RACING AND ENDURANCE CONTESTS

the fastest time to the top is the winner. These races cover distances from a few hundred yards to a few miles and make use of varied gradients.

In a massed-start race all the riders start at the same time and the first man to cross the finish line is the winner of the race. These races pit the riders against one another and are tests of riding technique and competitive ability as well as speed and stamina. The Tour de France, perhaps the best known bicycle race in the world, is a massed-start race which covers a distance of 2,600 miles from Lille to Paris. It is a grueling race and worthy of its reputation.

Cyclo-cross racing is a fascinating variation on the massed-start race. It is the cyclists' version of cross-country racing and it takes the competitors through areas that most people wouldn't even consider walking through. It may include fields, streams, bogs of mud, and even wooded areas. The cyclist must ride, carry, and even run with his bicycle in his attempt to best his opponents. Special bicycles are used for these races that are built and equipped to keep mud, sand, water, and tons of abuse from ruining the bicycle and preventing its rider from finishing the race.

RACING TECHNIQUE: To understand and appreciate cycle racing, you should have some knowledge of racing technique. There is more to racing than just speed and stamina. The cyclist who can outsmart his opponent will often win against a competitor who is stronger and faster.

There are three forces of resistance which reduce a cyclist's speed: air, road surface, and gradient. Road surface and gradient are factors which the cyclist has little control over. Correct gearing will certainly make a difference on hills, but the cyclist must still supply the power to overcome the grade. Air resistance is the factor that is of prime importance to the racing cyclist, and much is done during a race to reduce air resistance as much as possible.

The low body position used by racing cyclists does more

than just enable them to pedal properly. It also cuts down on the amount of air resistance. As a bicycle and its rider move along the ground, the air directly in front of the bicycle is relatively stationary and will resist movement through it. By crouching low over the handlebars a racing cyclist cuts through the air and cuts the effect of the resistance. The air in front of the bicycle is allowed to pass around and behind the cyclist with as little of the body meeting it head on as possible. An erect riding position would be like pedaling against a strong head wind.

When the air closes behind a cyclist who is maintaining a good steady speed, it leaves a wake, or quiet spot, directly behind where there is very little air, it having been pushed forward by the body of the rider. One technique used in racing to cut down on air resistance is for one cyclist to ride in another cyclist's quiet spot. This is called taking pace. The cyclist taking pace rides with his front wheel approximately six inches behind the rear wheel of the cyclist setting pace and experiences very little or no wind resistance. By keeping pace, a rider can pedal for hours behind the cyclist in front and use about half the energy to maintain the same speed. In this manner a cyclist can save his energy for the finish line.

Another technique used by racing cyclists is the surge. This is used when a rider who has been taking pace wants to pass the cyclist in front of him or when a rider who is back in the pack wants to drive into the lead. This has to be well planned and well executed if the rider does not want to end up with nothing but fatigue for his efforts. The surge is a sudden burst of speed which is usually planned to catch an opponent as much off guard as possible. To obtain this burst of speed the cyclist must lift off the seat, keeping his hips well forward and his back arched high, and pull on the handlebars with his arms and shoulders. This forces the entire weight of his body and the added strength of his arms and shoulders into the pedals. Both legs push and pull to obtain the highest spin rate possible. This is an all-out effort, and the trained

RACING AND ENDURANCE CONTESTS

cyclist will be using every muscle and every ounce of energy he has in his attempt to pass his opponent. Of course, the excitement comes when the rider who is being passed realizes what is happening and pours it on in turn.

Another sudden burst of speed called the jump can be used by a cyclist who wants to pull away from an opponent who is taking pace behind him. The jump is a sudden and violent thrusting forward of bicycle and rider. By lifting the weight of his body suddenly off the bicycle with his feet and arms, the rider can thrust the bicycle forward and then follow with as much of his body as possible. It is like trying to leap from the bicycle to a spot just ahead in the road, only once the rider has leaped, he takes his bicycle with him. All this is done without breaking the cyclist's steady pedaling rhythm.

Equipped with this knowledge of racing technique, you should try to see a bicycle race if you have never been to one. If you have seen one but didn't understand what was happening, go back and give it another try. There is much that the average cyclist can learn by watching the style and technique of the racing cyclist.

WHERE TO FIND RACES: Races are regularly publicized in many cycle magazines, organizational publications, and in some areas even in the more conventional media, such as local newspapers. If you are interested in racing, either as a participant or as a spectator, you should write to the Amateur Bicycle League of America, 4233 205 St., Bayside, Long Island, New York, and ask them where you can contact the ABLA official nearest you. He can supply you with information on how to get started in racing or where to go if you want to see a bicycle race.

Chapter 15

Camp Cooking

Although it is possible when traveling by bicycle to stop at restaurants and motels along the way, there are cheaper, more authentic, and more enjoyable ways to obtain food and shelter. Camping is by far the cheapest and most enjoyable of all the ways to travel. There is so little opportunity for direct contact with nature these days that any chance to rough it is well worth taking. Aside from stemming some of the drain on your pocketbook, camping can be a unique and gratifying experience. Even if you do not sleep in the wilds, by cooking there you can get some idea of what it is like to live in close contact with natural surroundings. Too much of our time is spent surrounded by steel and concrete. With the knowledge of campfires and camp cooking needed to produce a good meal from a minimum of supplies and some dry wood, you will be able to dine in the splendor of the great outdoors.

UTENSILS: Your cooking utensils should be kept at a minimum. Lightweight aluminum cooking kits can be purchased at sporting-goods stores with many utensils that fold together into one compact unit. One frying pan and one pot are usually adequate for a person to do all the cooking that will be necessary on the road. Most camp dishes can be prepared in one utensil, combining all the ingredients for a well-balanced meal into one convenient dish. Foil can also be used very effectively in place of cooking hardware.

FOOD: There are some basic considerations that should be kept in mind when selecting food to take along on a tour. It is a good idea to purchase some items near the area that you intend to use for a camping site, but much can be carried on the bicycle. Regardless of whether you take your own food or purchase it on the road, it should be well suited to the needs of a cyclist pedaling over long distances. Any food you choose should be easy to digest. This is wise since meals are sometimes rushed and usually followed by physical exertion. Food should be quick and easy to prepare. You don't want to use too much time in cooking meals. Bulky foods should be avoided and anything containing water should be left at home. By adding water to your food once you get to camp you will save yourself the trouble of having to carry it. Though it may not seem like it, water is quite heavy, especially when your bicycle is already loaded with necessary items. Foods that are likely to burn will cause much wasted time. Aside from the unpleasant experience of eating burned food, you will have the unpleasant experience of cleaning your burnt pot afterwards.

Remember that the less the weight and the higher the caloric content, the better a food item is for traveling! The average person needs 3,500 calories per day while out on the road. This caloric count can easily be contained in about 2½ pounds of food.

MEALS: *Breakfast:* A good breakfast is important to an active person. It should supply enough sustenance to get the day started with vigor and enthusiasm. A poor breakfast may result in a poor morning. While out on the road, an improper breakfast will make your cycling more of a chore than it should be and probably ruin your entire day, so don't skimp and you will have the energy you require to travel the miles you have to travel.

It does not take much time to fix the variety of items needed for a balanced breakfast. You should have at least three different types of foods and at least one of them should be hot. Dried fruit can be cooked in boiling water. Apples and apricots are the fastest and therefore the best to use if you want to get an early start. Fresh fruit or juice will do equally well. Instant orange juice will provide vitamin C. Dry or cooked cereal, hot cakes, toast, eggs, bacon (Canadian bacon is best since there is less fat on it), ham, spam, can all be eaten in any number of combinations. At least two of these items should be a part of your morning menu. For drinks, coffee and hot cocoa are a good warm way to start the day. Don't forget the leftovers from the night before. Meat, vegetables, and potatoes that weren't eaten for dinner can easily be used to bolster your breakfast dishes. Use a little imagination and the result may even be an amazingly tasty new recipe.

Lunch: Lunch should always be kept simple and concern should be given to speed and ease of digestion. It is not worthwhile to cook a lunch, so those foods that can be eaten cold are the best selections. Hot soup may be a good idea on a cold day, but for the most part sandwiches, cheeses, fruits, raw vegetables, and a drink of milk or cold juice will save you time and trouble.

Dinner: Dinner is the largest meal of the day. A main course should be selected and then accompanied with vegetables and a starch. A bowl of soup is a good way to start your meal. It will replace some of the liquid lost during the day and warm the body up a bit. It is also easy to digest and will not spoil your appetite for the main portion of the meal. Soups can be thickened with flour (pea flour, soybean flour, or white flour), powdered milk, or instant mashed potatoes for extra body. The main course should be fresh meat or fish if they are available. Dried, smoked, canned, or dehydrated foods can be used as well, but there is something more satisfying about fresh food for dinner. Rice, spaghetti, macaroni, noodles, mashed or baked potatoes should be served as the starch. For dessert, stewed fruit, cookies, jello (preferably with fruit mixed in), and instant pudding can be eaten. Remember to save any leftovers for the next day.

DEHYDRATED AND FREEZE-DRIED FOODS: Dehydrated foods make it possible for any cyclist to carry his own food supply and not be burdened by excess weight. Dehydrated foods take up very little space, last indefinitely without refrigeration, and yield many times their weight in prepared food. They are ideal for camping and are used as emergency rations by many people. Many advances have been made in recent years in the preparation of precooked foods. New freeze-dry methods have enabled manufacturers to produce foods that take up very little space and still have the taste, smell, and appearance of fresh food once they have been prepared.

Packages containing complete menus can be purchased that will eliminate a good deal of planning and trouble. Manufacturers have prepared units which you need only open and follow the instructions to produce fine meals with all the calories necessary for days on end.

In preparing dehydrated foods you should be careful not to cook them too fast. Burning and sticking are a problem. If the directions say to boil the contents of a package in water, bring it to a boil slowly. When bubbles start to form, simmer on low heat, preferably in a covered pot, and stir occasionally. Boiling too vigorously can destroy your meal. When the directions require soaking you should measure the water carefully and begin the soaking first thing when you get into camp. This will eliminate the frustrating experience of having to wait while a ravenous hunger wages war with your body. If it is possible to set the food in a warm place while it is soaking, it will speed the process, but you have to be careful that it is only warm and not hot. Foods that you are instructed to form a paste with should be put into a large bowl while you pour a measured amount of water slowly into the mixture. Try to eliminate all lumps and mix the ingredients thoroughly. Work with the paste until you have made it smooth and then the rest of the water can be added.

In cooking at high altitudes you have to be especially careful. Water evaporates faster at high altitudes than it does closer to sea level. You may have to add water from time to time to make up for what is lost in evaporation. Keeping pots covered will help to reduce the amount of water lost in the air.

Dehydrated foods can be purchased through sporting-goods stores and direct-mail outlets. Only those products sold by reputable manufacturers should be purchased. They use a better quality of food so that there will be less to throw away when you get to camp than if you use foods manufactured by less reputable firms. The amount of money you save on inferior products is always lost later on, when it is more serious. Here is a partial list of manufacturers who handle dehydrated foods.

Bernards Food Industries
559 West Fulton St.
Chicago, Illinois

Dri-Lite Foods
8761 Santa Fe
South Gate, California

Chuck Wagon
P.O. Box 66
Newton, Mass.

E-Z Food Products Company
1420 S. Western Ave.
Gardena, California

Megdem Industries
6808 Marshall Rd.
Upper Darby, Penn.

Seidel Trail Packets
97 Chambers St.
New York, New York

Trail Meals
J.B. Kilskey
1829 N.E. Alberta St.
Portland, Oregon

Tripperoos
Hilker & Bletsch
614 Hubbard St.
Chicago, Illinois

CAMP RECIPES: These recipes are basic suggestions. They should by no means be followed exclusively. In most camp cooking there is deviation from the prescribed ingredients due to a shortage of one item or an abundance of another. Do not forego a meal just because one of the ingredients is not available. Try substituting something else that is on hand and is similar to what is missing. You may be surprised to find that you have discovered a new and exciting taste treat. I will include some basic instructions, such as for cooking rice, as well as some specific recipes for delightful eating while on the road.

Rice: Rice should be instant unless you are willing to take the extra time necessary to cook brown rice. Rice should first be heated in butter before adding the recommended amount of water. If you want to add a little extra flavor you can also throw some dehydrated onions in with the butter. Once you have heated the rice you should add about two cups of water for every cup of rice if it is brown rice, and the recommended amount of water if it is instant. If you add a bouillon cube it will give your rice even more flavor. Simmer the rice over low heat and keep it covered. Cooking time will depend on the type of rice. Brown rice usually takes 45 minutes to an hour. Instant rice can usually be cooked in 15 minutes or less. If you have the time it is better to use brown rice. It has more flavor and more nutrients than instant. Almost all kinds of vegetables, fish, and bits of meat can be added to the rice to turn it into a deliciously healthy meal.

Noodles, Macaroni, and Spaghetti: All of these starches are cooked in basically the same way. Boil the dry ingredients in enough salted water to just cover them. Stir occasionally and add a little water at a time if it evaporates. Cooking time is usually around 15 minutes and you should taste the pasta to see if it is done after this time has elapsed. Grated cheese can be added when cooked to provide variety and flavor.

Hot Cereal: All cooked cereals are prepared by adding the cereal slowly to a measured amount of boiling water. The water should be well salted. The amount of the ingredients will vary, but you can try 1/3 cup of cereal, 3/4 cup of water, and 1/4 teaspoon salt per person. If more water is needed, you can add it while cooking. Be sure to stir constantly because these cereals have a tendency to stick. Do not get them too thick because they will continue to thicken even after you take them off the fire. If you want to add some dried fruit to the cereal, boil it for a bit before you add the grain.

Hot Cakes: The best method for preparing hot cakes is with prepared flour. All you have to do is add water, which saves time and trouble and gives you perfect hot cakes every time as well. Be sure to clean and grease the frying pan well. An unprepared pan will make it hard for you to turn the hot cakes because they tend to stick easily. When bubbles form on the top side of the hot cake it is ready to turn. Mixing instant mashed potatoes or bananas with the batter will add extra flavor. Hot cakes can be served with a syrup made by adding brown sugar to boiling water, with honey, or with jam.

Coffee: Instant coffee is the easiest and most convenient to use while camping. If you are an avid coffee drinker and can't bear the thought of instant coffee, you should boil the water and add regular grind coffee to it. Use two cups of water per person and two tablespoons of coffee per cup of water. When the water is the desired color you should take it off the fire and if you have any eggshells left over from breakfast you should throw them in. Let the grinds settle. If you don't have any eggshells you may have to strain the coffee when you pour.

Meat and Vegetables: A good method for cooking meats and vegetables, either separately or together, is in foil. Food can be wrapped before it is packed and when you get to camp all you have to do is place the foil-wrapped package in the coals of the fire and turn it now and then. For cooking meats, add a little grease on the foil to keep the meat from sticking and burning; for vegetables, a little water should be added.

Bread: It is possible to bake your own bread in camp. Prepared biscuit flour should be used to save time and trouble. Use just enough water to make an easy working dough. Then brush the loaf with more flour and grease some aluminum foil with butter or other shortening. Wrap the dough loosely so that the foil will not break open when the dough rises. Place the foil-wrapped loaf at the edge of the coals and turn it often so that the sides will be evenly heated and will not burn. For the last couple of minutes you can put the loaf in the center of the fire for a golden crust to form, but don't forget it or you will have burnt bread to eat.

CAMP COOKING

Fish: If you have taken your fishing license along and want something fresh for dinner, it is always a good idea to go out and catch your own fish whenever possible. Fish should be cleaned (the scales removed by scraping) and gutted. Bread them with flour and fry in a greased pan until golden brown. They can be served separately or cut up and added to a mixture of rice and vegetables.

Stews: Stews are the old camp standby and make a hearty meal that can be prepared with any bits and pieces of meat, vegetable, and potato that you happen to have around. You should dice the meat you are using and then dust it with flour. Brown the meat in butter and onions and then add enough water or beef broth to cover the mixture. When the water starts to boil you should add diced potatoes and vegetables (carrots are best for this dish). Add enough additional water to more than cover the ingredients and simmer until the meat is tender. Celery and green pepper are good vegetables to add to flavor. Fresh tomatoes will also give the dish another kind of taste, and a little bit of sour cream added just before taking the stew off the fire is a delightful touch.

Hash: Hash can be made from either beef or corned beef and boiled or mashed potatoes. Vegetables, onions, and any other ingredient that catches your fancy can also be thrown in. The meat should be cooked and then chopped up. Add this to your cooked potatoes with a little butter and a little water in a frying pan. Cook for a few minutes and then break an egg on top of the mixture. When the egg is cooked you can dish it out and serve.

Fruit: Dried fruit should be boiled slowly in water or eaten as it is. If you add sugar to your boiled fruit, do so just before you are ready to take it off the fire. Fresh fruit, such as bananas and apples, can be baked in foil for a delicious dessert. Baked apples are prepared by coring the apple and filling the hole with brown sugar. Bake the apple in greased aluminum foil until tender. Bananas can be baked with honey but should be cooked slowly.

Camp Kabobs: A good way to cook meat and vegetables is on a stick. Find a green stick about the size of a pencil and strip off the bark. Take your skewer and put chunks of meat, potato, onion, green pepper, mushroom, and tomato on it securely, and then prop it over the fire. Any kind of meat and any combination of the items listed can be used for a tasty meal.

Meat Pies: To make a meat pie, start as you would with a stew. Brown the meat in butter and onion and then add diced potatoes, vegetables, and enough water to cover the ingredients. Mix some biscuit dough and place it over the top of the ingredients. Cover the pan and set on the fire. When the dough is cooked, you are ready to eat.

Hot Dogs: There are many things that can be done to make ordinary hot dogs a gourmet delight for your camping menus. You can add flavor to hot dogs by cutting a slit down the side and filling it with cheese. Wrap this combination with bacon and fry until the bacon is crisp. Another treat is to mix some biscuit dough and roll it out as thin as possible. Cut pieces of dough large enough to wrap around the hot dog and still leave the ends open. Wrap in foil and bury in the coals for about fifteen minutes.

Potato Soup: Potato flakes make a marvelously easy soup. Just boil onions in water until tender and add about three times as much milk as water. Add potato flakes until the soup looks slightly thickened. You can add peas, whole potato, and pieces of meat to the soup to give it extra flavor.

Chapter 16

First Aid

A cyclist should always be careful, when riding, to prevent accidents. Nevertheless, they do happen, and when they do, he should be prepared to deal with them. Many people are seriously hurt every year because they do not have the basic knowledge of first aid needed to minimize danger after an accident. Everyone should know how to keep a person who has suffered injuries in the best possible condition until medical attention can be obtained.

Even if you should be unable to help yourself after an accident, a knowledge of first aid can be important so that you will be able to tell someone else what to do and what not to do. Even minor injuries can become rather serious if unattended or attended without the proper knowledge. If

THE PEDALER'S HANDBOOK

you must rely on someone else to take care of you in an emergency situation, you will be far safer if you can monitor their activities or instruct them as to how they can help you rather than make the injury worse than it already is.

DIAGNOSIS: Before any problem can be properly treated it must be properly diagnosed. An accurate evaluation of the injuries sustained in an accident should be the first order of business. If you are in an accident, you should try to remain as calm as possible. Even people suffering from severe wounds and shock can keep a cool head long enough to get themselves out of danger. This is essential. Panic will not keep anyone alive. Though most of the injuries encountered by bicycle riders are minor ones, there is always the possibility that serious problems will arise, and you should be prepared to deal with them when they do. Do what is necessary first and fall apart later. It could save your life.

Until you are sure there is no serious injury, assume that there is. Do not try to move unless there is further danger present. There are no bodily injuries that are made better by moving (with the exception of cramps) and most are only complicated further. There are times when moving an accident victim can be fatal. Stay put if possible. Take a few seconds to recover from what has happened and then start to evaluate the situation. If it is possible to summon help without moving, this should be done immediately. In most cases help will be readily available. Even someone who doesn't know anything about first aid can be a help if guided by someone who does. It is not always possible to diagnose your own ailments and an observer can always be of service.

The most immediate signs of bodily damage are pain, bleeding, and swelling, but their absence is not always an accurate indicator of the amount of damage. Strange as it may seem, you can feel perfectly fine, maybe only a little shaken up, and still be in serious danger. A fractured spine

FIRST AID

cannot always be felt right away, yet it can be paralyzing to move someone who has suffered one. Always check for symptoms, and move an accident victim, and this includes yourself, slow and easy. The time you take could mean many extra years of healthy life.

TREATMENT: Always treat those problems which are the most serious. This implies that you have to make an accurate diagnosis—and this is definitely the case. Just because you can see a wound that is bleeding does not mean that it should be attended to first. Some bleeding wounds are very minor and their treatment should never preempt the time for the treatment of more serious problems.

Unless you have sustained only minor cuts, scrapes, and bruises you should seek medical attention. First aid is not intended to cure most problems, only to keep them under control until someone who is more qualified can administer the actual treatment. Never be afraid to get professional help as soon as is possible after an accident. There are injuries that can go unnoticed and untreated for long periods of time, only to flare up more seriously than if they had been diagnosed and cured from the beginning.

MINOR WOUNDS: Small cuts, scrapes, and bruises are minor wounds. Just because they are called minor, they should not be neglected. The tiniest of cuts can go unnoticed due to lack of bleeding and still become infected or damage vital organs well beneath the surface of the skin.

Cuts and scrapes are breaks in the surface of the skin. The skin is a protective layer which prevents dangerous bacteria from entering the bloodstream. Even with a minor wound there is always the possibility of infection. Treatment for minor cuts and abrasions is basically designed to aid healing and, more importantly, to prevent infection.

All breaks in the skin should be washed and kept clean.

More serious injuries usually require further treatment, but for minor injuries, unless complications arise, keeping the wound clean is the only treatment necessary. The body will do the healing.

Minor cuts and abrasions should first be checked for the presence of foreign particles. Bits of glass, sand, dirt, and gravel should be carefully removed. Do not try to pry out any object that is lodged tightly; leave that to a doctor. Trying to force out material that is deeply imbedded could cause further damage and an increase in bleeding. Any bits of clothing should be kept free of the wound, and if there is any dead skin it should be cut away with a pair of scissors.

Once that you are sure the wound is free of foreign material, clean it with soap and water. If soap is not available, plain water will have to do. It may hurt a bit, but persevere. If the pain becomes unbearable, wait for a few minutes and then proceed again. Hands should be clean when handling injuries and any cloth used should be clean. Try to avoid breathing or coughing on an open wound. This may sound silly, but it is sound advice. The mouth is a breeding ground for germs and, although they are not normally dangerous, they can cause infection in an open wound.

When the wound is being cleaned it is also necessary to clean around the injured area. This will prevent any dirt in the proximity from coming into contact with the opening in the skin. Hold a cloth, or better yet a sterile pad, over the wound and clean out and away from it. Clean thoroughly; it could save you from serious danger.

Once the wound is clean and free of foreign particles, you should apply some form of antiseptic and a dressing. When you have applied the antiseptic, take a sterile pad and open it carefully. Try to keep your fingers away from the side which will be placed on the skin. Cover the wound completely and wrap gauze around the pad to form a secure bandage. This should prevent any bleeding and keep the wound free from infection while healing. Don't wrap the gauze so tightly that circulation is cut off, but firmly enough to stop any bleeding, and ensure that the bandage will stay in place. Apply tape to hold the gauze secure.

Puncture wounds can be deceptive. They are much deeper sometimes than they appear to be and can damage tissues well beneath the surface of the skin. If undue swelling occurs you should consult a doctor immediately and have the wound checked for more serious damage.

Bruises are caused by bleeding into tissue underneath the surface of the skin. Though they are not usually serious, they can be, especially as a person gets older. As in any bleeding wound, first aid for bruises consists in trying to stop the flow of blood. If you sustain a bad bruise, you should do as little physical activity as possible. Place cold compresses over the bruised area and, if the bruise is on a limb, raise it to slow the flow of blood into that area.

BLEEDING: Blood loss can be serious and no time should be wasted in getting medical attention if severe bleeding occurs as the result of an accident. The blood that has been lost must be replaced or it could be fatal. External bleeding can easily be seen and estimates easily be made as to how much blood has been lost. The swelling around broken bones is an indication of blood lost internally due to fractures. A broken thigh bone will usually result in the loss of two pints of blood, a broken shinbone one pint, a broken elbow a half-pint. Any combination of broken bones will result in a dangerous loss of blood, and the only effective treatment is an immediate transfusion. If internal bleeding is diagnosed, help should be obtained immediately.

It is not always possible to see whether or not a person is bleeding. Therefore you should be able to recognize symptoms of blood loss and assume that the victim is bleeding even though no blood or swelling is visible. The skin will look pale and be cold to the touch. It may also feel clammy since the person will be sweating slightly. The pulse will be rapid and weak. Take the pulse regularly (at five-minute intervals). If the pulse rate increases, the bleeding has not stopped. A record of the pulse rate will be beneficial to the doctors at the hospital in treating an accident victim, so if possible, keep a record.

First aid for bleeding should be an attempt to stop the bleeding if possible, minimize the amount of bleeding if it cannot be stopped, and prevent infection.

External bleeding should be stopped by applying pressure directly on the wound. If the wound is caused by a broken bone, you may have to apply the pressure around the wound so that you won't aggravate the fracture. Once pressure is applied, the flow of blood will stop and the blood can clot naturally to close the wound. Use a sterile pad or clean cloth if available; if not, the fingers of your hand will suffice.

Once the bleeding has stopped, apply a dressing to the wound. If the wound continues to bleed through the dressing, do not remove the dressing. Put an additional pad and bandage on directly over the first. Once the dressing is in place it should not be disturbed.

The injured person should be kept as still as possible. Activity increases the flow of blood and disturbs the process of clotting. If the bleeding is from an arm or leg, elevating the limb will also help to reduce the flow of blood. If bleeding has been severe, and if other injuries are not aggravated by doing so, the lower limbs should be raised. This will allow the blood to flow more easily into the areas that are vital for the sustenance of life, the heart and brain.

If you should be by yourself and suffering from loss of blood there is always the possibility of fainting. If you have a bleeding wound and feel faint, lie down on your stomach with your head slightly turned to one side. Try to lie so that the weight of your body will continue to apply pressure to the wound even after you will have lost consciousness.

There is no way to stop internal bleeding. The only first aid that can be given is to keep movement at a minimum until the person can be taken to a hospital for treatment. People with chest injuries should remain in a sitting or half-sitting position until arrival at the hospital. If internal wounds occur in other areas of the body, the person should be taken to the hospital lying down.

Nosebleeds are rarely serious. They can occur spontaneously or as the result of an injury. High altitude can cause nosebleeds in some people. First aid consists of resting with the head higher than the rest of the body and pinching the front of the nostrils with your fingers until the bleeding has stopped.

A black eye is actually a form of internal bleeding. Applying an ice pack in the early stages can reduce the amount of swelling and pain. Black eyes are not usually considered serious, but they should be checked by a doctor. Any blow that is serious enough to cause a black eye could also have caused other damage to this sensitive area.

FRACTURES: A fracture is a broken or cracked bone. It can be an open fracture, in which case the bone has penetrated the skin, or a closed fracture, in which case the skin is not broken. If it is an open fracture there is the same danger of infection which is present in any wound and it should be treated accordingly.

Recognition of fractures is not always easy. In a closed fracture, the break will not be seen except as an abnormal shape due to unusual bone placement or swelling around the fracture. Pain is usually severe and becomes worse if the affected area is moved. There is usually a loss of muscular ability in a broken limb and the limb may hang limp. Broken bones can also be felt to grate against one another in some cases when moved and the broken ends can sometimes be felt underneath the skin.

Open fractures should be covered to prevent infection, but

care should be taken to disturb the protruding bone as little as possible. Never try to put the bones back into their original positions. That is a job for a doctor with the proper training and equipment. Any movement of broken bones will result in great pain and possibly further damage.

You should immediately immobilize any fracture. The victim can be placed in any position that feels comfortable and causes least pain to the affected area. If it is necessary to move a broken limb, traction should be applied by pulling the limb away from the body. Keep traction steady until the limb can be secured; to release it would cause extreme pain. A broken arm should be fixed to the body to keep it stationary. A broken leg can be tied to the other leg. The body makes a very effective splint and should be used when needed. When binding limbs in position care should be taken to pad any hollow spots that will cause the limb to fit irregularly and increase the possibility of damaging movement. In limbs, breaks should be immobilized above and below the nearest joints.

Broken limbs should be checked regularly to make sure that swelling does not cut off blood circulation. If the skin starts to turn color, becoming white or blue below the break, or if there is a loss of feeling below the break, blood circulation is probably being impaired. All bandages should be loosened and the limb should be straightened if there is loss of circulation. Be sure to tell the doctor that the circulation had slowed when the person gets to the hospital.

If more than one limb has been broken, a major bone has been fractured (such as a thigh bone), or if there are broken bones present with loss of blood from other wounds, there will be urgent need for a blood transfusion and the victim should be taken to a hospital by the quickest available means. Remember that any broken bone has a loss of blood associated with it and with some bones this loss can amount to as much as four pints.

Extreme care should be used if you suspect that someone has a fractured spine. The spine protects the spinal cord and if the spine is fractured there is danger present to the spinal cord with the slightest movement. If the cord should become pinched or severed, paralysis could occur throughout the entire body. There will usually be pain at the site of the fracture and the injured person will appear anxious and pale. However, it is possible that a person who has a fractured spine could feel perfectly calm and relatively free from pain. Breathing may be difficult and, in some cases, the victim may be unconscious. If there is any evidence of paralyzation in the limbs, the possibility of a fractured spine is very strong and the victim should not be moved.

Speed is the least important factor in the first aid necessary for a fractured spine. There will be no swelling and very little loss of blood. The most important concern should be with preventing further damage. The person should not be moved at all until the ambulance has arrived. If there is no ambulance available help should be obtained. It takes at least four people to move one person with a broken spine safely. When lifting the victim onto a stretcher, a blanket should be used. Roll him carefully on his side, holding the head to minimize movement. Slide a half-rolled blanket underneath the body, and then roll the person on top of the blanket. Once the blanket is underneath the victim, roll up the sides to get it as close to the body as possible. When lifting onto a stretcher, two helpers should pull gently on the head and neck for traction.

DISLOCATIONS: Dislocations occur only at joints. The bone is displaced from its normal position in the joint and the muscles and ligaments which normally hold the bone in place may be torn. First aid for dislocations is basically the same as that for fractures. Cover any open wounds, prevent further injury by immobilizing the area, and send the person to a hospital. Do not try to replace the bone in its original position; this will cause further damage.

Pain is usually severe at the site of a dislocation. There will be swelling and the person may feel sick. Dislocations can usually be recognized by the deformity caused when the bone leaves its normal position. The bone will be held in the position you find it by a contraction of the muscles. Movement of the affected area will be severely painful and should be avoided.

Keep the victim comfortable and transport him to a hospital as soon as possible. Check for the impairment of circulation as with fractures. If circulation has stopped, loosen all dressings and straighten the limb. Upon arrival at the hospital inform the doctor that circulation has been impaired.

SNAKE BITES: A non-poisonous snake bite should be treated like any other puncture wound. Wash the area thoroughly and apply a sterile dressing. No further treatment should be necessary unless infection is noted. There are four types of poisonous snakes in the United States: Pit vipers, which include rattlesnakes, copperheads, and cottonmouth or water moccasins, that inject venom into the bloodstream through two puncture holes creating immediate pain and swelling; and the coral snake, which is smaller and chews rather than bites, whose venom affects the nervous system rather than the bloodstream, and which can also inject tetanus germs into the body. The bite of a coral snake causes a burning sensation and very little swelling. Non-poisonous snakes cause very little pain and almost no swelling beyond what is normal for any puncture wound.

Absorption of the poison from snake bites brings on nausea and vomiting, general weakness, and shortness of breath. The pulse becomes weak and rapid and sometimes vision may dim. These symptoms appear quickly if the

FIRST AID

poison is injected directly into the bloodstream, but may take up to a couple of hours to develop. The fatality rate for untreated snake bites is not very high, but there is a fatality rate, so treatment should always be administered.

When bitten, a person should stop all muscular activity immediately. The best method of first aid is to draw the poison out of the body through the same place that it was injected. A constricting band should be tied above the bite on arms or legs. This should be tight enough to slow the returning blood, but should not cut off the circulation of blood flowing into the limb. Crosscuts must be made on each puncture with a sterilized knife. The knife can be made sterile by passing the blade through a flame. Cuts should be made shallow when cutting across a limb so that the blood vessels and nerves that lie beneath the skin will not be damaged. Longitudinal cuts can be made slightly deeper.

Once the cuts have been made, suction should be applied. This can be done with suction cups designed specifically for this purpose or it can be done with the mouth. Venom is not harmful to the digestive tract so there is no danger in swallowing; but the mouth should be washed out regularly since any openings from sores or cuts will cause some discomfort when the venom comes into contact with them. Suction should be continued for an hour and then the victim should be taken to a doctor. During periods of rest from drawing out the venom an ice pack will help to reduce swelling and slow the absorption of the poison.

ANIMAL BITES: Animal bites carry germs from the animal's mouth into the body. Because of this, the greatest danger is from infection. Tetanus and rabies are always an added possibility. Bites should be cleaned, as with any wound, and a dressing applied. A doctor should always be consulted to ensure that there is no danger from rabies or tetanus.

It is helpful if the animal can be held for examination. If signs of rabies appear then the victim of a bite must undergo the painful experience of rabies inoculations. If the animal can be proven to be free of rabies, then the victim will be spared shots. Rabies is fatal if not treated, so all bites from warm-blooded animals should have medical attention.

HEAT STROKE AND HEAT EXHAUSTION: Heat exhaustion will cause muscle cramps and profuse sweating. The pulse will be rapid and weak. Although there is generally no loss of consciousness, a person will feel dizziness and will be extremely weak. Someone suffering from heat exhaustion should be taken to a cool place and should have complete rest. Body heat should be maintained. No attempt should be made to cool the body down, only to keep it from becoming overheated. Sweet or saline liquids should be given by mouth.

Heatstroke occurs when the heat-regulating mechanisms of the body are overwhelmed. The onset is often rapid and consciousness is lost in severe cases. The face will be flushed and the skin will feel hot and dry. The pulse will be strong and rapid and the person may feel dizziness and nausea. Medical attention is required for anyone suffering from heatstroke. While waiting for transportation to a hospital the person should be taken indoors and rested. Sponge baths should be administered to keep the body temperature down to less extreme levels. Saline liquids should be given to a patient if fully conscious, but only in small amounts. Heatstroke is serious and the person should be hospitalized at once.

EXPOSURE: Persons who have been subjected to prolonged periods of cold will show signs of abnormal behavior. Apathy, dreaminess, difficulty in movement, and slow response to stimuli are symptoms of exposure. Excessive drowsiness is experienced and the person may be unconscious

FIRST AID

or semiconscious. There may also be muscle cramps and loss of sensation in the body.

Treatment consists in finding shelter for the victim immediately. He should be warmed with blankets or a warm bath. Hot water should not be used; it will produce too strong a shock on an already damaged system. If no bath is available, placing the hands and forearms in warm water will help. When the person is conscious hot liquids should be drunk. Keep the person dry and covered because the body will lose heat rapidly.

FIRST-AID KIT: First-aid kits should be carried with your bicycle at all times. Even a ride of a few blocks can be marred by an accident, and quick and immediate action may have to be taken. Many kits are sold on the market and almost all are suitable for carrying as long as they don't take up too much room and have at least the basic items needed to administer first aid. If you plan to tour or camp with your bicycle, it is probably better to purchase a larger kit than you would ordinarily carry. If injuries occur while out on the road, the extra items will be well worth their weight. A basic first-aid kit should include the following:

- 1½" x 5 yd. roll of adhesive tape
- 1" roll gauze bandage
- 6 3-inch sterile pads
- Iodine
- Aspirin
- Bandaids
- Blunted scissors
- Triangular bandage (can be used as a sling or as a bandage)
- Tweezers
- Small writing pad and pencil

Chapter 17

Dos and Don'ts

To get the most from your days of happy cycling, you should get involved. There are many ways in which you can learn how your bicycle runs, how to run your bicycle, and just about anything else that you will ever need to know about a bicycle. Books and magazines are useful in getting you started, but the only way to master the art and science of cycling is to spend time with your bicycle.

One really fine way to become an expert cyclist is to associate yourself with people who have already spent years becoming experts themselves. The various associations and clubs which promote and sponsor bicycle rides are full of cyclists who have the experience and willingness to help the novice learn all that he will need to know to get years of enjoyment from his bicycle.

The League of American Wheelmen is a good bicycling organization for those interested in touring. The local Wheelman clubs sponsor regular rides which usually cover distances from 25 to 100 miles. The rides are well planned, well supervised, and well executed. If you want to tour you would do well to tag along as a guest of the Wheelmen for at least one ride so that you can get the feel of riding long distances. If you are looking for good cycling routes and a chance to learn more about cycling, you would do well to participate in the three rides necessary before joining, and then join. The membership fees are only $6.00 a year for one person, $7.00 for a couple, and $10.00 for an entire family. It will be a good opportunity for you to learn more about cycling from people who have already been riding for many years.

KNOW YOUR BICYCLE: Even if you never make any major repairs on your bicycle, you should have some knowledge of how to keep it in good running condition. Even a cursory knowledge of bicycle maintenance will come in handy when you have to take your bicycle to a repair shop. You may not be able to fix the bicycle, but you will be able to talk to the people who will. If you know how a bicycle should perform, you will be better able to notice things that are amiss before they become serious.

A knowledge of how your bicycle works will also help you to be a better cyclist. Understanding the principles of gearing, ankling, climbing hills, etc., will help you cycle more efficiently and with greater benefit than those who never bother to discover what cycling is really like. If you know how to use and take care of your bicycle, it will offer you many years of riding pleasure.

HOW TO HANDLE A BICYCLE: A fine-quality bicycle should be handled properly at all times. A bicycle is not a

DOS AND DON'TS

toy, nor will it stand up to abuse. More than just a good look at the bicycles owned by some of the children in the neighborhood will bear this out. Children ride their bicycles harder and are less careful with them than most adults. Even though these bicycles are built to withstand an amazing amount of punishment, they do not last long if ill-treated.

A bicycle is made to stand upright on two wheels. It should never be left lying on its side. The only time a bicycle should be set on the ground sideways is when making repairs, and even then it is better avoided. Dirt and damage can ruin your hubs, spokes and crank. The handlebars and pedals also usually suffer when laying or dropping a bicycle on its side.

Derailleur mechanisms are expecially sensitive and must be handled delicately if you want them to stay aligned and adjusted. It is easy to bend the derailleur by dropping the bicycle or hitting the derailleur unit on something while riding. An extended rear axle nut on the derailleur side might help somewhat to keep it safe, but nothing will keep it running correctly like proper handling.

You should also try to avoid bumping the derailleur gear-shift levers when handling your bicycle. Derailleur gears were designed to shift while the bicycle is in motion. Bumping the levers can cause damage to the unit. You should never shift the levers yourself, or let anyone else do so, when the bicycle is not in motion and the pedals are not turning.

CURBS AND OTHER ROAD HAZARDS: Curbs are personally responsible for the ruin of more rims every year than most people would suspect. Many cyclists are too lazy or in too much of a hurry to go the extra few feet needed to find a sloped entrance to the territory beyond the curb. Being this lazy, and a bit foolish besides, they will often ride right up and over the curb. This is quite a shock to the front wheel of a bicycle and should be avoided. You can quickly ruin a rim and, if you dent it, it will have to be replaced.

To prolong the life of your tires and rims you should be constantly on the alert for bad road surfaces or obstacles in the road. A large crack in the concrete pavement can cause considerable damage to your front wheel if hit at a high speed. Rocks, stones, and other debris in the road should also be bypassed.

If you cannot avoid going over a rough surface, it is a good idea to rise up off the seat of the bicycle. This will more evenly distribute your weight along the bicycle and enable your arms and legs to act as shock absorbers for the bicycle. It will also produce less of a jolt to your body.

DOGS: Dogs present a rather peculiar problem to the cyclist. There is something about a bicycle in motion which seems to annoy even the friendliest of dogs to the point of immediate attack. There are many devices that have been developed to combat this age-old foe, and the cyclist should be aware of them. He should then choose one with which to arm himself.

Some cyclists carry a tiny whip mounted on the handlebars with which to fend off attack. It can be quickly plucked from its holder and used on the nose of the dog, thus convincing him that he should return to his own territory and leave the road to the bicycle riders. This requires a bit of skill with both whip and bicycle. To actually discourage a dog of any agility and size whatsoever you will have to master the art of the whip while in mortal combat, with only one hand on the handlebars. Even if mastered you run the risk of infuriating the animal still further and having him gobble you up whip and all.

Another handy dog repeller comes in a spray can. It is a pepper derivative that can spray about ten feet and will stop any dog. The effects are not lasting, but they are powerful when administered. The spray can is rather hard to store and keep within reach, however. By the time you have the can of

DOS AND DON'TS

spray out of a saddlebag, the dog can have his teeth in your leg.

Perhaps the best way to outsmart a dog is to outrun it. If the dog hasn't cut you off, pour on the power and whizz by him before he can catch you. Do not try to outrun a dog unless you think you have a really good chance of making it. Aside from biting a rider, dogs have also been known to get their noses caught in a rider's spokes. At a good speed this can cause a bad spill.

In most cities it is illegal to let a dog run loose. If you have one in your neighborhood that is constantly giving you trouble, it would be well worth your while to find the owner and inform him of the regulations on loose dogs in your city. If the owner does not take the proper steps to ensure you a safe ride, you can contact the government agency responsible for enforcing the regulations.

ITINERARY: When traveling by bicycle it is always a good idea to let someone know what your itinerary is so they have a fair idea of where to locate you if an emergency should arise. If you are going on a short ride and will not be gone for more than a few days, you should notify your family or a friend of your intended route and time schedule. If you are going camping or touring along less traveled areas of the country it is always a good idea to let the local authorities know of your plans and where you intend to be. In this way, if anything should happen, someone will have an idea of where to find you. They will also be able to give you current information on conditions in the area you wish to travel through or camp at.

PROPER SPIN: Studies have shown that the cadence range for maximum efficiency on a bicycle is between 55 and 85 revolutions per minute. The importance of maintaining a regular spin that lies somewhere within and preferably in the higher ranges of these revolutions cannot be stressed enough. A good rhythmic pedal spin will greatly reduce the cyclist's fatigue and enable him to travel long distances with a minimum amount of effort.

Your gears should be used to enable you to maintain your spin. You should not slow down on the pedals when shifting a derailleur and if you do so on a hill you will not be able to shift into a lower gear. You should never try to force the gear. Try to shift before you actually have to slow your spin down. You should practice shifting properly from the start, which means shifting while the pedals are turning at the proper number of revolutions per minute to allow a nice easy slip of the chain from one sprocket to another. This will keep your derailleur from damage and keep your spin at a consistent speed.

Chapter 18
Keep It Clean

In order to keep your bicycle in good shape and add years to your enjoyment of trouble-free riding, it should be cleaned and cared for regularly. Like any precision piece of machinery your bicycle should be maintained to keep it in good running condition. A bicycle contains many moving parts that must be lubricated regularly to minimize wear and drag. Your bicycle must be checked periodically for worn parts and, if found, they should be replaced. Loose bolts, wheels that are out of line, and faulty brake parts can mean costly damage if not corrected soon enough. Fixing your bicycle once it has broken down is no substitute for proper upkeep when it comes to getting the best possible performance.

CHAIN MAINTENANCE: Your bicycle chain is the means by which the power supplied to the pedals is transferred to the rear hub and, in turn, to the wheel. As the pedals turn, friction is created at those points where the chain rolls on the front and rear sprockets. To reduce this friction, thereby increasing the life of the chain and reducing the amount of drag it causes, you must keep the chain well lubricated and free of dirt. If the chain is not well greased, you can also cause irreparable damage to the sprockets in an amazingly short period of time.

There are many theories as to the best possible lubricant to use on a bicycle chain. Grease has been used for years as a standard lubricant, but paraffin wax and modern petroleum distillate sprays are also used by many cyclists. Regardless of what you use, the chain should be removed, cleaned, and relubricated regularly. If old grease and dirt are allowed to build up for too long, you will find yourself replacing the chain and the sprockets.

To remove the chain on a single- and three-speed bicycle requires only a pair of pliers and a screwdriver. You will have to find the "master link" on your chain. This is done by checking both sides of the chain carefully for a link that is wider than the rest and has a clip over the chain rivet that holds the face of the link in place. This clip can be removed by forcing the open end of the clip open slightly and sliding it back until it is free of the rivet. The link can then be disassembled and the chain can be removed from the sprockets.

If you have a derailleur-type gear changer you will not be able to find a master link on your chain. The extra width of a master link will not fit through the derailleur cage so there is no master link. You will have to have a riveter-extractor to remove your chain. This tool, which can be purchased for about $2.00, is specially made for removing and replacing the rivets in a chain link.

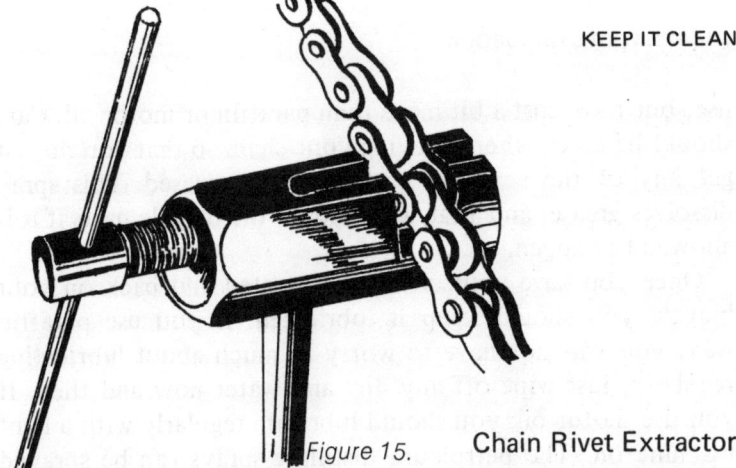

Figure 15. **Chain Rivet Extractor**

Once the chain is removed it should be dipped in solvent. Paint thinner and kerosene are the best solvents to use since they are not as volatile as gasoline. If you do use gasoline, make sure that you do so in a well-ventilated area. Leave the chain in the solvent long enough to remove all the old grease and dirt. Dip the chain in and out repeatedly to help loosen the accumulated material. When the chain looks clean, hang it up to dry.

This cleaning should be performed about once every two months unless you ride often or have occasion to travel through dirt and sand, in which case it should be done more frequently. This will prevent rust and keep the moving parts of the chain as free as possible from damage.

To relubricate the chain you can use either No. 10 motor oil, hot paraffin wax, or a petroleum distillate spray. You should try several different methods to see which you are happiest with. If you use motor oil, dip the chain in the oil and then rub off all the excess before replacing the chain. Paraffin is probably the cheapest lubricant. It is also tougher than motor oil and will attract less dirt. You must heat the paraffin before dipping in the chain, and after coating the chain you will have to hang it up so the paraffin can harden. You can save the leftover paraffin and use it again, so don't throw it out. The petroleum distillate sprays are handy to use, but they cost a bit more than paraffin or motor oil. Care should be taken when spraying your chain so that you do not get any of the spray in parts that are greased. This spray dissolves grease, and that will damage the bicycle parts if it is allowed to happen.

Once you have your chain relubricated and back on your bicycle you should keep it lubricated. If you use paraffin wax, you will not have to worry as much about lubricating regularly, just wipe off any dirt and water now and then. If you use motor oil, you should lubricate regularly with a light machine oil. The petroleum distillate sprays can be sprayed on occasionally.

BEARINGS: Bearings are small steel balls that fit in between the bicycle frame and the turning parts such as wheels, cranks, heads, and pedals. These steel balls keep the turning parts from rubbing directly against one another and causing wear.

To find your wheel bearings you will have to remove the wheel and the axle nuts. Just inside the axle nuts, next to the hub, there is another set of nuts. Loosen these, and then carefully remove both the nuts and the axle. This will free the bearings rather suddenly so be careful to do it in an area where you are not liable to lose any. Place the bearings, axle, and nuts in a can of solvent. On the inside of the hub there is a groove in which the bearings turn. This should be thoroughly cleaned with the end of a rag which has been dipped in solvent. When you have the groove cleaned and all the parts are soaked clean and dried, you are ready to repack the wheel bearings with grease. High-quality grease can be obtained at any auto-parts or bicycle shop, the former being much cheaper. Fill the bearing groove with the grease, and place one-half of the bearings in either side of the hub, arranging them so that they are, more or less, equidistant from one another. The grease will be thick enough to hold the bearings in place while you reinstall the axle and the bearing keepers to their original positions. Tighten the nuts with your fingers until they are snug. Test the axle by hand to make sure that it turns freely. If it is hard to turn, the bearing keepers are too tight. If it wobbles they are too loose and should be tightened. Make sure that you wipe all excess grease off the outside of the hub before you reinstall the wheel. After the wheel is in place and properly centered, take a test ride to make sure that all is well.

To clean your crank bearings you will first have to remove your crank. If you have a one-piece crank assembly, you should remove the left pedal by first turning the bottom bracket locknut in a clockwise direction. You will then have to remove the lock washer, the adjusting cone, and the ball-bearing retainer cage which contains the bearings. Next take the bearing retainer out on the chainwheel side and slip the entire assembly out through the right side of the bottom bracket. Clean, regrease, and reinstall the assembly. Be careful when you tighten the adjusting cone not to get it too tight. If it is too tight the crank will not turn freely.

If you have a European bicycle or an American bicycle with a European crank, it will be either a cottered or a cotterless crank. To remove a cottered crank you will have to remove the cotter key which holds the crank in place. The nut that holds the key in place should be turned a few times. After it is loose, hit the pin gently with a hammer and punch, but be careful not to ruin the threads on the key or damage the bottom bracket. Once the cranks are loose you can remove the lockring on the bottom bracket. When you remove the lockring, bearings will fall out all over, so be careful not to lose any. Be especially careful not to let any bearings fall down into the tubular frame. If they do you will have quite a job on your hands trying to retrieve them. Once the bearings are free, clean, regrease, and reinstall the entire assembly.

To remove European cotterless cranks you will need special tools that fit the brand of crank you have on your bicycle. These tools should be purchased when buying the bicycle. You will have to be careful with cotterless cranks because they are not made of steel and using too much leverage when removing them is liable to ruin the threads, forcing you to replace the crank (an expensive task).

The crank tool is designed to remove the crank nuts and then extract the crank from the axle. You may have a hard time removing them, even with the extractor, since they are usually tight. If you have trouble, give the extractor a light tap with a hammer and then turn it slightly. Keep up this procedure, alternating taps and turns until the cranks come loose. Once you have removed the cranks, you can service the bearings and reassemble. If you apply a light machine oil to the threads of the crank you will not have as much trouble the next time you have to remove them.

To clean and regrease the bearings in the steering system you will have to start by removing the handlebars. Loosen the stem bolt a couple of turns and tap it with a hammer. This will loosen the handlebar stem and it can be removed. Next loosen the locknut on the top of the headset and the washer. Remove the adjusting cup and you can pull the fork out of the bottom. Remove any bearings that are left in the top or bottom cones and clean the cones with solvent. After the parts are clean, regrease and reassemble the head.

Pedals also have bearings that need regular cleaning. If you have conventional pedals, you should first unscrew them by turning the left-hand pedal clockwise and the right-hand pedal counterclockwise. Remove the two small nuts at the threaded end of the pedal axle and pull out the metal bracket which holds the rubbers. Next pull out the axle assembly. Unscrew the locknut and the adjustable cone will come loose, freeing the bearings inside. Clean, regrease, and reassemble the pedals.

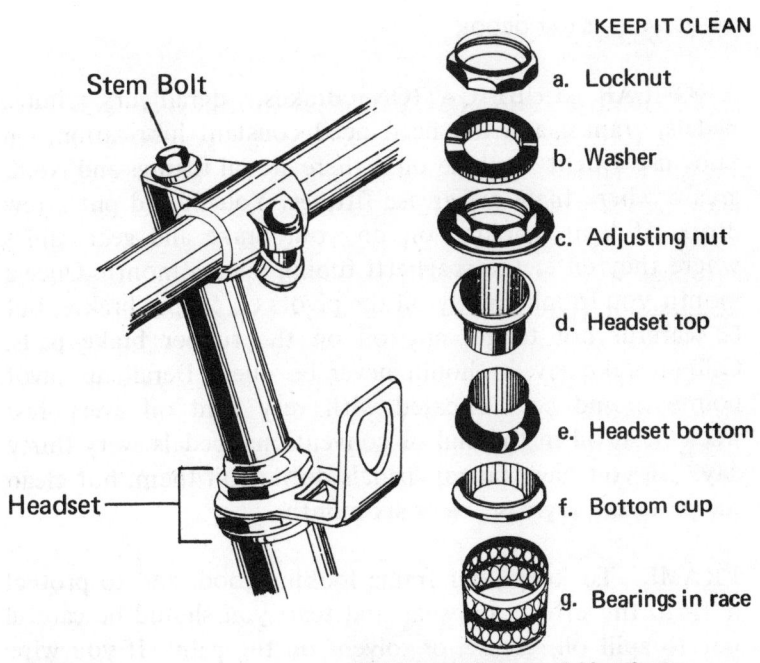

Figure 16. **Exploded View of Headset**

If you have rattrap pedals, you will not have to remove the pedals to get at the bearings. Just remove the dust cap and you can reach the adjusting cone. The rest of the procedure is the same as for conventional pedals.

If you have a derailleur rear sprocket cluster it should be removed and cleaned regularly. Remove the freewheel with a freewheel remover and soak the entire sprocket cluster in solvent. It is quite a job to remove and regrease the bearings inside the gear cluster so you may want to leave this job to a bicycle repair shop. If you take your freewheel in fully cleaned, they will only have to repack the bearings and it may save you some money. This can be done at home if you are good at remembering how to put things back together once they are taken apart, but the freewheel contains parts other than bearings which must be replaced properly, so, unless you are sure of your abilities, leave it to someone with more experience.

REGULAR LUBRICATION: Brakes, derailleurs, hubs, pedals, cranks, and the head need constant lubrication. On hubs use a light machine oil if there are oil fittings and No. 2 grease where there are grease fittings. You should put a few drops of light machine oil on your brake and gear cables where they enter the spaghetti tubing once a month. Once a month you should lightly oil the pivots on caliper brakes, but be careful not to get any oil on the rubber brake pads. Caliper-brake levers should never be oiled. Derailleur pivot points should be lubricated with very light oil every few weeks. Put oil in the end of conventional pedals every thirty days. If you have rattrap pedals do not oil them, but clean the parts and regrease every six months.

FRAME: To keep your frame looking good, and to protect it from the effects of wear and tear, you should be careful not to spill oil, grease, or solvent on the paint. If you wipe your bicycle frame occasionally with a rag, especially after making repairs or riding in rainy weather, it will keep your finish looking like new. The paint is not only put on a bicycle for its outward appearance, it also protects the frame metal from rusting and corroding. If you are careful not to ruin the paint, you are not likely to ruin the metal underneath.

BATTERIES: If you have accessories on your bicycle which require the use of batteries, you should check the batteries regularly to see that they are still good. Once a battery is dead it can corrode the terminals on the inside of the accessory. If you haven't had any occasion to ride your bicycle with the lights on since the last time it rained, you may have ruined them. It is a good idea to remove your batteries whenever you are through riding and to store them in your saddlebag so you won't forget them the next time you go out. This way there will be no chance of dead batteries being left in place and destroying your equipment.

KEEP IT CLEAN

TIRES: Proper care of your tires will not only keep them running longer, it will keep them running smoother as well. The most common cause of tire damage (other than punctures due to sharp objects) is underinflation. Tubes and tires are made of rubber and any stress that they receive other than what they were built to receive will soon wear them out. Tires are designed to take the friction of the road on the outside tread. Any rubbing or bending of the sidewalls of the tire will produce cracks and eventual deterioration.

To keep your tires properly inflated, you should invest in a tire gauge. In a pinch you can judge the inflation of your tires by feeling how hard they are, or by watching to see how much the tire bulges while riding. If the tire bulges excessively, it is underinflated and it will receive stress on the sidewalls which were not meant to take it. With a tire gauge you can inflate the tire to the minimum recommended inflation with accuracy and consistency.

When you fill your tires there are other factors to consider besides the recommended pressure. On a cool day it is safe to inflate to the maximum pressure recommended for the tire, but on hot days the heat from the air and the heat caused by the friction on roads will cause the air inside the tire to expand considerably. This could cause a blowout, so if the temperature climbs, reduce the pressure in your tires by about five pounds.

If you are heavier than average, or if your bicycle is packed with touring or camping equipment, you should increase the air pressure in your tires to approximately five pounds over the recommended minimum pressure. Make sure when you ride that there is very little bulge where the tire meets the road.

Your tires should wear evenly. If you notice that the tread is wearing unevenly, you must find the something that caused it and remedy the problem. Check to see whether your brakes are adjusted properly. Crooked rims may also be a cause of uneven tread wear, so you should check regularly to see that your rims are straight.

Tires can be inflated either at a service station or with your own bicycle pump. If you inflate your tires at a service station, you must be careful not to overinflate. Service-station pumps can fill a bicycle tire in seconds and, in a few more seconds, burst it. You should fill the tire with air in short spurts, checking after each spurt to see how much the tire has been inflated. With a hand pump you will not have to worry about overinflation, but be careful not to damage the valve by excessive movement of the pump once it is in place. When removing the pump from the valve, give it a sharp blow with your hand rather than wiggling it from side to side. This will help to prevent valve damage.

You should also be careful not to inflate your tires to maximum pressure on a cold night and then bring them into a warm house. The heat inside the house will cause the air inside the tire to expand and you could have a blowout. Let a little air out of the tires before going from cold air to hot air.

Tubular tires lose a little air daily. The walls of the tube are thin enough to allow air to seep through them very slowly. This air has to be replaced, so a few strokes with a hand pump every day will keep them at the proper inflation.

Tubular tires should not be left folded in the same position for long periods of time. If left rolled up they will develop weak spots along the creases of the fold. Remove, inflate, and let tubulars stand for awhile about every four weeks. When refolding make sure that the folds are not the same as when you last folded the tire. Keeping your tubulars in plastic bags folded once will also help to keep them dry and prolong the life of the tire. Make sure when strapping tubulars behind your seat that they are not rubbing against anything that will cause weak spots or punctures.

Whenever you adjust or replace spokes be sure to remove the tire and tube from the rim. The spoke heads can protrude through the rim and cause a puncture. Always file down any protruding spoke heads flush with the rim after adjustment.

STORING YOUR BICYCLE: If for any reason you wish to store your bicycle for any length of time, care should be taken to do it properly. A bicycle can be damaged as easily by not riding it for long periods as by riding it all the time. If you are going to store your bicycle you should try to do so in a place that is dry and has as little variation in temperature as possible.

Never store a bicycle that isn't clean. Dirt and grease should be removed before placing it in storage. Parts should be regreased and the bicycle should be well oiled if you are to prevent moisture from rusting it while it is not in use. Even though it is in storage, it would be a good idea to take the bicycle out regularly and service it. Grease and oil drain out of the various parts if allowed to sit for any length of time.

Store the bicycle with some type of protective cover if possible. A bike cover will work well. If you can seal the cover it will add an extra bit of protection against the effects of moisture.

When you take your bicycle out of storage you should grease and oil all of the parts that require lubrication before you start to ride. Grease and oil drain out of hubs, cranks, and derailleurs if left to sit for long periods of time. Your bicycle will not have proper lubrication after being taken out of storage just because it was lubricated before it was put in.

Chapter 19

Protect Your Property

Coupled with the tremendous growth in bicycle sales, this country has witnessed a substantial increase in bicycle thefts. The stealing of bicycles has become a very lucrative business that can quickly rob you of your cycling pleasure. Most cities have waged an all-out war on bicycle thieves, but their ranks continue to grow and thieves snatch thousands of bicycles each week from the hands of unsuspecting or unprepared cyclists. If you want to keep your bicycle safe, sound, and in your possession you will have to arm yourself against the would-be spoiler of your bicycle happiness.

Even if your bicycle is stolen, there are certain procedures that you can follow to recover it. It is possible for the police to recover stolen bicycles if they are given a little help by the owner.

CHAINS: A good-quality chain and a good-quality lock will not necessarily stop a bicycle thief, but it will provide a good deal of discouragement. In most cases discouragement is enough to send a smart thief in search of easier prey. Chains come in all shapes and sizes, and are made from a variety of different metals, but most of them are, in the end, rather worthless. It takes a good, thick, hardened steel chain to withstand a simple chain-cutting tool. Putting any of most of the bicycle chains currently on the market on your bicycle will leave it a prime target for the highly professional bicycle thief.

Cables should be avoided. They are not strong enough to withstand the most primitive of chain destroying devices. Cables are light and inexpensive so many cyclists do use them, at least until their bicycle gets stolen for the first time. Then they invest in a sturdier form of protection.

The chain you select should be at least ¼ inch thick and made from hardened metal. Chains that are not hardened will not afford any protection. It should be three to four feet in length to make it useful for fastening your bicycle to a variety of objects. It may take some looking around to find a suitable chain, especially if you want one that is thicker than those normally used. If you want a thicker chain as well as the security gained by using one, you will have to find a department or hardware store with a good selection of case-hardened chains.

LOCKS: As with the chain, your lock should be sturdy enough at least to slow down the typical bicycle thief. Your good chain will not do you a lot of good if the thief can simply force the lock. The lock should have a shackle made from at least ¼ inch hardened metal and a key.

The lock should be a good-quality key padlock. Combination locks should be avoided. The key-type padlock is far sturdier and harder to force open than combination locks.

PROTECT YOUR PROPERTY

One-piece combination-lock and chain assemblies are worthless and should not be used. If you want help in picking out a lock, you should go to a local locksmith and have him explain the different locks and their advantages and disadvantages. You can then pick the one that you feel will give you the best security.

HOW TO USE A CHAIN AND LOCK: You should always chain your bicycle to something that is firmly attached to the ground. Bicycle racks, trees, telephone poles, fences, outside water pipes on buildings, etc., can be used to keep your bicycle sitting in the same spot as you left it. Never assume that passing your chain through one wheel and the frame, thus preventing the wheel from turning, will stop a bicycle thief. This is an ostrich approach to protection. Just because the bicycle cannot be ridden does not mean that it cannot be stolen. Most bicycle thieves are perfectly willing and able to carry a bike away chain and all.

You should loop your chain around the stationary object that you have selected; then pass it through the rear wheel *and* the frame. Remember that anything that isn't tied down is liable to be carried away. A bicycle thief is not above spending the time to remove your wheel and then walking off with the frame and front wheel.

For double security it is a good idea to use two chains whenever possible. This will enable you to secure both wheels and the frame to a stationary object and lessen the chance of losing any of the three.

ACCESSORIES: If you are riding somewhere and will have to leave your bicycle unattended, it is best to keep as many accessories at home as is practical. Once you have arrived at your destination, you should carry as many with you as you can carry. Accessories are generally easy to remove and even easier to carry off. If you must leave them out somewhere, you will just have to hope that nobody is working in that area whose line is bicycles.

PARK SAFELY: One of the factors that you should always consider when you park your bicycle is just how easy you are making it for the bicycle thief to work. A dark street or alley will suit a thief's purposes very well. He needs the cover of darkness and the privacy it affords to complete his intended business if he is to have your bicycle. When choosing a place to park your bicycle look for a spot that is well-lit and well-traveled. If there is a large amount of foot traffic in the area you will stand a better chance of having someone spot the bicycle thief and summon help. It is also better to leave your bicycle well away from the side of the road if possible. The farther a thief has to carry a bicycle to put it into his automobile, the less likely he will be to attempt the feat.

You should seek out satisfactory parking locations for your bicycle. Even if you end up walking an extra block, the extra protection it will give you will make the walk worthwhile.

LICENSING: It is always a good idea to register your bicycle with the local police. A bicycle with a license will be much easier to recover than one that is not registered. If it is licensed, it will usually be returned to the owner immediately upon recovery. It is also a good idea in case you should be involved in an accident. Police can use the bicycle's license number in much the same way that they use automobile license numbers to discover who should be notified. The time it takes to register your bicycle will save much precious time in an emergency situation.

FRAME NUMBER: If your bicycle is stolen you will have to report the frame number to the local police. Every bicycle owner should know what his frame number is to be able to

PROTECT YOUR PROPERTY

find it if the bicycle is stolen. Bicycles are identified by their frame numbers since these numbers are permanently stamped on the bicycle. The theft will have to be reported as soon as possible for there to be any chance of recovery.

MARKING YOUR BICYCLE: There are two ways that you should mark your bicycle. Some mark or marks should be made that are obvious to anyone who will try to steal it. If a bicycle thief has to remove identifying marks from the frame and rims, he may move on to bicycles that will be easier to get rid of.

The bicycle should also be marked in some secret way to aid in identification if it is every recovered after having been stolen. It will also help if you should happen to see a bicycle that looks like yours in the hands of someone else after it has been taken from you. This may sound like a foolish bit of movie-style espionage, but it is really a good method for making a positive identification if the need ever arises.

A good method for protection is to stamp your driver's license number into the frame with a metal punch. Driver's licenses are a fast form of identification and can be checked by police in a matter of minutes. If you do not have a driver's license, you can use the number of another member of your family. If you stamp it into more than one place it will be a little more difficult to remove and it may make a thief reject your bicycle as too risky.

Chapter 20

Traveling with Your Bike

If you have been traveling by car or some other means of transportation, you will probably benefit from carrying your bicycle with you the next time you go somewhere. Although not everyone will become an avid enthusiast for the effort and planning required for a bicycle tour, you can take it with you to wherever you are going, and thereby get more enjoyment from the area you are visiting. Taking your bicycle along on a trip will enable you to get around without having to worry about an automobile or public transportation. Bicycles make it possible for you to explore areas that you would never be able to see by car and would not be able to spend the time seeing on foot.

If you are traveling abroad, don't forget your bicycle. It is a convenient and inexpensive means of transportation and in foreign countries where bicycles are in greater use for transportation, you can get around with ease and safety. Considering the problems in driving an automobile in a foreign country and the legal entanglements that can arise if you should ever have an accident, your bicycle will be a good, safe means of transportation. You will see much more than if you were to walk from place to place and it will give you greater mobility than an automobile in most countries. It will also put you in closer contact with the people of the country that you are visiting.

CAR CARRIERS: Anyone who has ever struggled to cram his bicycle into the back seat or trunk of the car can testify to the advantages of having a car carrier. If you happen to live in a city, a car carrier is almost a must. It will enable you to transport you and your bicycle out of the populated areas and into the countryside where you can ride with relative freedom and safety. If you already do any amount of traveling by automobile, a car carrier will make it easy for you to take your bicycle along on those vacation or weekend trips. Even a trip to the repair shop is greatly facilitated if you can just strap your bicycle onto your carrier and not have to worry about how you are going to take enough of it apart to fit into your automobile.

Car carriers come in two basic types and each has its advantages and disadvantages. Bumper carriers are the most widely used since they are easier to lift a bicycle onto and are adequate for most cyclists' needs. Carriers that mount on the top of the car or on the trunk are a bit more difficult to use since it is necessary to lift the bicycle much higher than with the bumper carriers, but they can carry up to four bicycles at one time while most bumper carriers can only accommodate two. It would probably be wise for a bicycling family to

TRAVELING WITH YOUR BIKE

invest in a top carrier since it will be needed to carry the family's collection of bicycles. One other factor that should be taken into consideration when choosing the type of carrier you will want is the amount of wind resistance that the bicycles will cause when you are driving. If you have a small car, you would be better off with a bumper carrier since bicycles mounted on the top will cause problems when driving on windy days.

An adequate and inexpensive bumper carrier is a "Bike-toter," that sells for approximately $12.95. "Tote-a-bike" is a better carrier, but it is a little more expensive at $21.95. "JCI" is a good brand of roof carrier, and starts at $29.95 for a two-bicycle carrier. It will run another $5 for each additional bicycle, up to four, that the carrier can accommodate. "Garard" roof carriers are also good at approximately the same price. If you have a station wagon, a good carrier is the "American Eagle" collapsible carrier. This carrier collapses, affording access to the rear gate without having to be removed. The "American Eagle" costs $29.95, but is worth the investment if you have need for it.

REMOVABLE WHEELS: If your bicycle is equipped with quick-release hubs, you may not even need a car carrier. With these special hubs you can greatly reduce the bulk of your bicycle by removing the wheels. With the wheels and frame separated you should be able to fit the bicycle easily into the trunk of your car. The wheels should not be placed in a position where they are likely to receive any spoke damage and the tires should not be allowed to rub against any wood or metal while being transported. If the tires rub against anything, it will cause weak spots in the rubber. Make sure that there is no chance for the frame to fall over on the wheels. It is a good idea to place a piece of cloth over the frame to separate it from the wheels.

AIRLINES, RAILROADS, AND BUSES: If you were to call any airline, railroad, or bus company, you would get a pretty standard reply on questions about the procedure for taking your bicycle with you on a trip. Most companies will encourage you, rather forcefully I might add, to ship your bicycle as freight. This of course means that you will have to pay the going rate for shipping freight. If you are traveling any distance, this could amount to a substantial sum of money.

Though taking your bicycle by bus is difficult to do without paying the freight charge, it is possible to get away with it on airlines and railroads. The enforcement of rules on the airlines and railroads is not consistent and depends mostly on the people you have to face at the baggage check. It is possible to wheel your bicycle up to the baggage clerk and have him put a baggage tag on it for you. If you should succeed this far, you should also ask him how to get to the person responsible for loading your bicycle. When you get to the loading area you should personally supervise the handling of your bicycle to make sure that nothing is damaged.

To prepare your bicycle for shipment you should remove the pedals and turn the handlebars parallel to the frame. This will make the bicycle more compact and will keep it from damaging other baggage when in transit. This may also help you to win points with the people who handle your bicycle and points will aid you to get away without paying a freight charge.

On overseas flights it will be more difficult to take your bicycle along with you. Most overseas flights have strict limitations on the amount of weight a person can carry as baggage and you will have enough problems just keeping your luggage under the limit. If you are traveling overseas, it would probably be wise to ship your bicycle separately. Make sure that you plan the shipment so that your bicycle and you will arrive at approximately the same time.

TRAVELING WITH YOUR BIKE

Before your trip begins, you should investigate the rules and regulations of the airline, railroad, or bus line in regard to bicycles. You may find some companies that have accommodations for bicycles. If not, you should ask what the charge is for freight and be prepared to deal with that if you cannot slip past the personnel.

Chapter 21

Checklists

BUYING A BICYCLE: Features to look for when you are buying any bicycle—listed according to quality with the highest quality first.

    FRAME: Double-butted, alloy steel, seamless
Straight gauge, alloy steel, seamless
Double-butted, rolled steel with seams
Straight gauge, rolled steel with seams

JOINTS:	Lugged and brazed Fitted welded
FORKS:	Tubular, alloy steel Non-tubular, rolled steel
BRAKES:	Center-pull Side-pull Coaster
PEDALS:	Conventional rubber tread Touring Racing
RIMS:	Lightweight aluminum alloy Steel
TIRES:	Tubulars Clinchers
CRANK:	Cotterless Cottered One-piece
GEARS:	Derailleur gear mechanism Multispeed rear hub
HANDLEBARS:	Turned down or flat Raised or high rise
HUBS:	One-piece machined with wide flange Stamped metal
SPOKES:	Double-butted Straight gauge
SADDLE:	Racing or touring Spring type

CHECKLISTS

CHECK IT OUT FOR A TRIP: A bicycle should always be checked thoroughly before you start on a trip. This checklist will help.

DERAILLEUR ALIGNMENT:	Chain tension Sprocket clusters Chain cage high and low stops Shift-control levers
CABLES:	Brake cables not worn or bent Derailleur cables not worn or bent
CHAIN:	Well greased No broken or loose links No excessive wear
BRAKES:	Brake pads Brake adjustment
LUBRICATION:	Hubs Pedals (except rattrap) Pivot points on brakes Crank Head set Derailleur pivot points Derailleur freewheels
SPOKES:	Proper tension None missing or worn
RIMS:	Straight No dents
SEAT:	Height adjusted Well broken-in
HANDLEBARS:	Adjusted properly Knurled section not worn

THE PEDALER'S HANDBOOK

    BEARINGS: Recently regreased
                          Not worn excessively
                          Not frozen

    WHEELS: Alignment in fork
                          True roundness
                          Free turning, no binding

PLANNING A DAY TRIP

    CLOTHING: Riding jersey
                          Riding shorts
                          Riding shoes
                          Extra shoes or slippers
                          Pair of long pants
                          Windbreaker, unlined
                          Cap with visor
                          Raincape
                          Sunglasses
                          Gloves

    PARTS: Spare tube (or two sew-ups)
                          Spare brake cable
                          Spare gear cable
                          Spare brake pads (2)

    TOOLS: Tire patch kit
                          Two tire irons (for clincher tires only)
                          Mafac tool kit
                          6-inch crescent wrench
                          Small screwdriver
                          Pair of offset pliers
                          Freewheel remover
                          Chain riveter-extractor
                          Tube of bicycle grease
                          Spoke wrench

CHECKLISTS

ACCESSORIES: Lights with spare batteries and bulbs, where applicable
Chain and lock
Bike cover
Water bottle and mounting bracket
Tire pump
Toe clips
Reflectors
First-aid kit

CAMPING AND EXTENSIVE TOURING

CAMPING EQUIPMENT: Down sleeping bag (not waterproof)
Tent (sewn-in floor and mosquito netting)
Air mattress or foam pad
Waterproof matchbox
Camp stove and fuel (if you're going to use one)
Dish towel
30-foot nylon cord
First-aid kit
Sewing kit
Insect repellent
Can opener
Mess kit
Frying pan
Pot
Compass
Canteen

CLOTHING: 2 pairs socks
2 pairs underwear

1 pair extra shoes or slippers
2 long-sleeved nylon sport shirts
1 light wool or loose-knit shirt
1 pair wool mitts
Windbreaker
Raincape
2 pairs cycling shorts

TOILET
ARTICLES: Toothbrush
Toothpaste
Soap (wrapped in plastic)
Washcloth
Towel
Razor and blades (where applicable)
Comb
Mirror (stainless steel)

SPARE PARTS: Same parts as day trip with the exception of six brake pads and two gear and brake cables
Spare chain
6 spokes

TOOLS: Same as for day trip

Chapter 22

Appendix

AMERICAN YOUTH HOSTEL ASS'N. (AYH) OFFICES

Arizona
Arizona State Council
4634 E. Lewis
Phoenix 85008

California
Golden State Council
625 Polk St.
San Francisco 94102

Los Angeles Council
318 N. La Brea Ave.
Los Angeles 90036

Northern Calif. Council
P.O. Box 15649
Sacramento 95813

San Diego Council
7950 Eads Ave.
La Jolla 92037

San Gabriel Valley Council
215 West 1st St.
Claremont 91711

Connecticut
Fairfield County Council

P.O. Box 173
Southport 06490

Hartford Area Council
YMCA, 315 Pearl St.
Hartford 06103

New Haven Council
48 Howe St.
New Haven 06103

District of Columbia
Potomac Area Council
1501 16th St., NW
Washington, D.C. 20036

Illinois
Metropolitan Chicago Council
3712 N. Clark
Chicago 60613

Massachusetts
Greater Boston Council
251 Harvard St.
Brookline 02146

Michigan
Metropolitan Detroit Council
14335 West McNichols Rd.
Detroit 48235

Minnesota
Minnesota Council
P.O. Box 9511
Minneapolis 55440

Missouri
Lewis and Clark Council
12201 Blue River Rd.
Kansas City 64146

Ozark Area Council
2605 South Big Bend
St. Louis 63143

Nebraska
Nebraskaland Council
2740 A St.
Lincoln 65802

New York
Metropolitan New York Council
535 West End Ave.
New York 10024

Syracuse Council
735 S. Beech St.
Syracuse 13210

Ohio
Columbus Council
P.O. Box 3165
Columbus 43210

Lake Erie Council
2000 Terminal Tower
Cleveland 44113

Lima Council
Box 173
Lima 45802

Toledo Area Council
5320 Fern Dr.
Toledo 43613

Pennsylvania
Delaware Valley Council
4714 Old York Rd.
Philadelphia 19141

Pittsburgh Council
6300 Fifth Ave.
Pittsburgh 15232

Wisconsin
Wisconsin Council
P.O. Box 233
Hales Corners 53130

CYCLING ORGANIZATIONS

Amateur Bicycle League of America
4233 205th St.
Bayside, Long Island, New York

American Youth Hostels, Inc.
20 West 17th St.
New York, New York 10011

Bicycle Institute of America
122 East 42nd St.
New York, New York 10017

British Cycling Federation
26 Park Crescent
London W1
England

Canadian Youth Hostels Ass'n.
268 First Ave.
Ottawa, Ontario
Canada

Cyclists' Touring Club
Cotterell House
69 Meadrow
Godalming, Surrey
England

League of American Wheelmen, Inc.
5118 Foster Avenue
Chicago, Illinois 60630

International Bicycle Touring Society
846 Prospect Street
La Jolla, California 92037

National Bicycle Dealers Association
29025 Euclid Ave.
Wickliffe, Ohio 44092

BICYCLE PARTS AND ACCESSORIES

Big Wheel, Ltd.
310 Holly St.
Denver, Colorado 80220

H.W. Carradice
Northstreet, Nelson
Lancashire, England

Cyclo-Pedia
311 North Mitchell
Cadillac, Michigan 49601

Metropolitan New York Council
American Youth Hostels, Inc.
535 West End Ave.
New York, New York 10024

Wheel Goods Corporation
2737 Hennepin Ave.
Minneapolis, Minnesota 55408

Youth Hostels Association
29 John Adam St.
London WC2
England

BOOKS ABOUT BICYCLING

American Youth Hostels' North American Bike Atlas, Warren Asa, (New York, Hammond, Inc.).

Anybody's Bicycle Book, Tom Cuthbertson, (Berkeley, California, Ten Speed Press).

The Complete Book of Bicycling, Eugene A. Sloane, (New York, Trident Press, 1970).

The Complete Cyclist, Harold Moore, (London, Sir Issac Pitman & Sons, Ltd., 1960).

Cycle Racing, Ken Bowden and John Mathews, (London, Temple Press Books, Ltd., 1965).

Cycling Handbook, A. L. Pullen, (London, Sir Issac Pitman & Sons, Ltd., 1960).

Cycling Manual, R. John Way, (London, Temple Press Books, Ltd., 1967).

Hostel Guide and Handbook, American Youth Hostels, Inc., New York.

How Many Hills To Hillsboro, Fred Bauer, (New Jersey, Hewitt House).

The Turned-Down Bar, Nancy Baranet, (Philadelphia, Dorrance and Company, 1944).

Index

Accessories 23-26, 74-75
baby carriers 28
bags and panniers 27-28, 74-75
baskets 28
compasses 30
first aid kit 76
horns 25-26
lights 24-25, 75-76, 174
odometers and speedometers 29-30
thefts of, prevention 181-182
tools 30-32, 76
weight of 23, 74
Accidents: see First Aid
Advantages of cycling 3, 7
Automobiles 4, 7-8, 64
Axles 122

Brakes 11, 73
adjustment 174
arms 118
cable 73, 116-117
center-pull 20
checklist for buying 192
coaster brakes, repairs 115-116
hand brakes, repairs 116-118
lubrication 115
mechanism 20
pads 117-118
quality, comparative 20
side-pull 20
Buying a bicycle 11-13, 21
checklist 191-192
dealers' shops 3, 11
department/discount stores 21
used, general check for 104-105
used, itemized checklist for 99-107
used, where to buy 105-107

Cadence: see Pedals; see also Gears
Camping 79-80, 137
checklist 195-196
cooking 137-146

THE PEDALER'S HANDBOOK

Carrier or rack for bicycle 8
Chain
front wheel 16
repairs 119-122
teeth 16
Checklists for
camping 195-196
day trip 194
long-distance trip 193
purchase 191-192
Children 12
Clothing: see Cycling, clothing
Clubs 56, 68-70, 171-172
Amateur Bicycle League of America 130
as places for repairs 110
Components, list of manufacturers 17
Cranks 40
checklist for buying 192
Compagnolo 19
cottered 19
cotterless 19
maintenance 171-172
one-piece 19
tools for 35, 171-172
Cycling
ankling 40-41
body position 39-40
clothing 33, 62, 75-77
conditioning and warm up 45-48
etiquette 65-66
handling 162-163
hazards 63-64, 163
hills 43
learning techniques 37-44, 161-163
night-time riding 62, 75-76
rain and fog 63
traffic 49-50, 62

Derailleur: see Gear changers
Disadvantages of cycling 8-9
Disease, relationship to cycling
vascular 5
heart 5-6, 46
Doctors 7, 46
Dogs 164-165
repellers 164

English racer 12, 13, 16
Exercise 4-5, 45-61
for racing 54-57
program for cycling by age 52-53

First Aid 147-159
accidents 147-149
bites 156-157
bleeding 151-153
diagnosis of injury 148
dislocations 155-156
exposure 158-159
fractures 153-155
heat stroke 158
kit contents 159
minor wounds 149-151
symptoms 148-149
treatment 149
Food: see Camping, cooking
Forks: see Frames
Frames
checklist for buying 191-192
maintenance 174
quality 7
racing 130
size 13, 16
style 19
tubing 17-18

Gear changers; see also Gears
derailleur (ten speed) 12-14, 16-19, 44, 72, 127-128, 133, 163, 166
derailleur repairs 111, 118-122
multispeed hub 127
Sturmey Archer multispeed hub repairs 118
Gears 11, 123
cable 102
cadence 126-127, 165-166
principle of 124-126
ratios 16, 126
selection of 126, 166
shifting 127-128, 166
shifting for hills 43-44, 124, 128, 132, 133, 136
size 16

Handlebars 11, 21, 34, 44
adjustment 73
maintenance 172
Health 4, 5-7
circulation of blood 5
lungs 6
Hosteling 83-90
accommodations 86-88
Hub (of wheel) 20

INDEX

Licensing: see Thefts, prevention

Maintenance 162-164, 167
bearings 170-173
chain 168-170
cover, use of 34
cranks 171-172
derailleur rear sprocket 173
frame 174
lubrication 174
pedals 172-173
steering system 172
tires 175
tools 34-36
Maps: see Routes, choice of
Muscles 6, 16
for racing 55-57

Parking 8, 182
Pedals 16, 19, 31-32, 40-44, 75
cadence 126-127, 165-166
checklist for buying 192
revolutions 124-125, 127-128
spin, proper 165-166
toe clips 42-43
tools 35
Pleasures of cycling 3, 6-9
Pollution 4
Price of bicycles 11, 13, 19

Races, locations 135
Racing 129-135
road racing 132-133
techniques 133-135
track racing 130-131
training 54-57, 132
Tour de France 133
Repairs 21, 65, 110-122
axles 122
coaster brakes 115-116
cost 109
derailleur gears 110-111
do-it-yourself 109-110
flat tires 111-115
hand brakes 116-118
multispeed hub 110-111
professional 110-111, 116, 162
tools 30-32, 34, 110-122
wheels 122
Rim of wheel 21
checklist for buying 192

maintenance 175-177
racing 130
tools 35
Road shock, absorbing 17
Routes, choice of
itineraries 165
local 67-69
long distance 78-79
maps, sources for 68-69, 93
maps, topographical 92-95
maps, use of 91-97
Rules of the road 59-66

Saddles 21, 73-74
Safety 8, 62-65
equipment check 59-60
nighttime precautions 62
Sightseeing 7-8
Speeds 12-13, 72
single 12
multispeed hub 12
ten 12-13
Spin: see Pedals
Sprockets 119-120, 124-127
maintenance 173
size 14
Storage of bicycle 177

Tensions, relief of 4, 6-7
Thefts, prevention of 179-183
chains and locks 180-181
identifying marks 184
licensing 183
Tires 11, 21
checklist for buying 192
clincher 112-113
flat 111
maintenance 175-177
pumps 30
racing 113-115, 130, 176
repair 31, 111
Touring 55-57
checklists 80
clubs 56
food 77-79
preparing bicycle 72-74, 193
trips, American Youth Hostel
    Association 88-90
Traffic 4, 7-8, 62
regulations 59-61
road signs 60

turning signals 60
Transportation, bicycle as 3, 4, 185
commuting on 12
Travelling with bicycle
abroad 185-186
car carriers 186-187
removable wheels 187
shipping 188-189

Trips: see Touring

Weight (of bicycle) 12-13
Wheels
repairs 122
removable 187
size 14
tools 35